# OLYMPICS

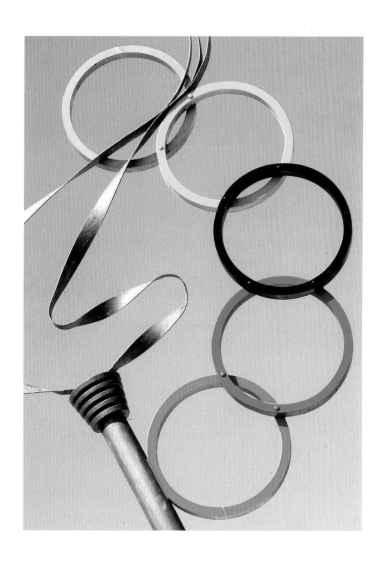

igloo

# OLYMPICS

## igloo

Published in 2011
by Igloo Books Ltd
Cottage Farm
Sywell
NN6 0BJ

www.igloo-books.com

B044 1111

2 4 6 8 10 9 7 5 3 1
ISBN 978-0-85780-249-1

Cover images provided by Corbis

The pictures in this book were provided courtesy of the following:
Getty Images, 101 Bayham Street, London, NW1 0AG

Nick J Webb, Brunel University, Conservative Party,
Why Oh Gee, AE Books

Written by Jon Stroud

Distributed in association with G2 Entertainment Limited
Printed and manufactured in China

# Contents

# Adlington

Not many people are appointed an Officer of the Order of the British Empire at the age of 20. Then again, at that age not many have already won two Olympic gold medals, equalled a 100-year-old national record or smashed a world record of 19 years' standing, either.

You can file swimmer Rebecca Adlington under all four headings. She became the darling of British sports fans in 2008 when, at the Beijing Games, she won gold medals in two events, rewriting the record books in the process. The OBE honour followed the following year.

The Mansfield-born Adlington was making her first Olympic appearances at Beijing, and she served notice of her intent when she posted a new Commonwealth record for the 400m freestyle in the heats.

The following day her first gold materialised as her time of 4.03.22 forced American Katie Hoff into second place. Adlington had become the first woman to win Olympic gold for Britain since Anita Lonsbrough nearly 50 years before.

The 800m freestyle, a few days later, went even better. In the final, Adlington demolished the field, as well as the longest-standing world record on the books, and finished in 8.14.10 – an extraordinary six seconds in front of second-placed Alessa Filippi.

She had quickly become a national hero, and swimming fans needed little reminding that the last time a British swimmer had won more than one gold medal had been 100 years previously, when Henry Taylor had claimed three.

# Ainslie

Sailing is in Ben Ainslie's blood, a fact to which four Olympic medals – three gold, one silver – bear testament. His father Roddy was a skipper in the 1973-74 Whitbread Round the World Yacht Race, and the young Ben was forever in or around boats as a child.

Soon his interest turned into something more serious, and Ainslie was a mere 16 years old when he became Laser Radial world champion. And the victories in single-handed sailing continued to pile up until the Olympics Games beckoned.

Competing in the Laser class at the 1996 Atlanta Games, where the sailing events were held off the coast of Savannah, Georgia, Ainslie finished second behind the Brazilian Robert Scheidt. He had won Olympic silver at the tender age of 19. He went one better four years later in Sydney, holding off Scheidt's challenge to claim gold, again in the Laser class.

By this time, Ainslie was looking to move up a class, which meant he had to gain 15kg in body weight. The change to the larger Finn craft made little difference, and at Athens in 2004 he was in gold medal-winning form again, denying Rafael Trujillo of Spain and Mateusz Kusnierewicz of Poland.

Beijing in 2008 presented different challenges. Winds and strong tides at Quingdao made conditions tricky and, with terrible timing, Ainslie contracted mumps just before the start of competition. But all that made little difference as he sailed home in the Finn class ahead of American Zach Riley and Frenchman Guillaume Florent. He had become Britain's most successful Olympic sailor ever.

# Aquatics

**RIGHT** An example of a team's free synchronised swimming routine

There are four areas of Olympic competition referred to as aquatics: swimming, diving, water polo and synchronised swimming.

The first Olympic swimming events took place at the inaugural Athens Games of 1896 in the open waters of the Bay of Zea, on a course marked out by floating hollowed-out pumpkins. Hungarian Alfréd Hajós, inspired to take up swimming following the death by drowning of his father, became the first Olympic swimming champion, winning the 100 metres freestyle in 1:22.2. A more unusual swimming event was the 100 metres freestyle for sailors which, not surprisingly, received a limited number of entries.

An expanded swimming programme at the 1900 Games in Paris produced a series of incredibly fast times, influenced largely by the fact that they were swum in the River Seine with the assistance of the current. Events included a 200-metre obstacle race and underwater swimming, in which marks were awarded dependent on time and distance.

Women's events were introduced at the 1912 Stockholm Games, with a limited competition consisting of the 200 metres freestyle and 4x100 metres relay. It was not until the 1924 Paris Olympics that a wider selection of events was launched.

Olympic swimming events are no longer held in the open sea or fast-flowing rivers! An Olympic pool must be 50 metres in length with eight marked lanes. Competitors are required to swim preliminary qualifiers.

In events of 400 metres or over, the eight fastest qualifiers advance to the final while in shorter events 16 qualifiers then compete in

a semi-final, with eight then going forward. The fastest qualifiers are then placed in the centre lanes of the pool for the final as these experience less water turbulence than those at the edges.

Rules governing false starts are strict. No competitor is penalised in any way in the event of a first false start, but after subsequent false starts the offending swimmer is automatically disqualified, whether they were guilty of the first false start or not.

Diving events always attract a great deal of interest at the Olympic Games. There are two forms of competition – springboard diving and platform diving – and they are contested individually and as synchronised pairs, with events for both men and women.

In springboard diving, competitors dive from a flexible board no less than 4.8 metres long and 0.5 metres wide fixed three metres above the water, while platform diving is performed from a rigid platform at least six metres long and two metres wide suspended 10 metres above the water.

Seven judges score each dive, with the result being multiplied by a difficulty coefficient that reflects the complexity of the dive performed.

Water polo is a tough physical sport played between two teams of 13 players, although only seven players from each team, including the goalkeeper, are in the water at any one time. The game is played over 28 minutes split into four seven-minute quarters within a field of play 30 metres by 20 metres.

The object is to score a goal by putting the ball between the posts of the opponent's goal. The ball may be played with any part of the body except a clenched fist.

In Olympic competition, men's and women's medals are contested in separate tournaments.

Synchronised swimming, seen by some as a rather trivial sport, is in fact incredibly demanding both physically and mentally, with athletes expected to combine strength, stamina and ballet like grace. Olympic synchronised swimming takes the form of a pairs competition and a team event for teams of eight swimmers.

Two routines are performed in each discipline. The first is a technical routine comprising set manoeuvres while the second is a free routine in which the creativity and choreography of the swimmers is put to the test. Both are scored by a panel of five judges.

# Athens 1896

With an estimated 80,000 spectators filling Athens' newly restored Panathenic stadium and most of the 245 competing athletes arranged by the 14 nations they represented filling the infield, these words, uttered by King George I of Greece, heralded the opening of the Games of the First Olympiad. The date was 6 April 1896.

The first competition of the inaugural games was the opening heats of the 100 metre dash. The American athletes proved outstanding with Frank Lane of Princetown recording a time of 12.2 seconds in that initial round and quarter mile specialists Thomas Burke and Thomas Curtis taking the subsequent two with identical times of 12.0 seconds. The "unusual" crouched start of these two Bostonians caused much interest with the European audience. Four days later it would be Burke who took victory in the final by two metres from Germany's Fritz Hofmann, once again recording 12.0 seconds.

The honour of becoming the first Olympic Champion since the 369AD victory of Armenian boxer Prince Varasdates fell to another Bostonian. Born to a poor Irish-American family, the 27-year-old self–educated Harvard freshman and US triple jump champion James

Connolly outdistanced popular Frenchman Alexandre Tuffère by over a metre.

What should have been a wonderful moment of triumph for the young American was somewhat tainted, however, by the crowd's frosty reception to his endeavours. Having dominated the preceding 100 metre heats, the Americans were not the flavour of choice for

**BELOW** The Olympic stadium in Athens, 1896

**BELOW** The start of
the 100 metres sprint
at the first Olympic
Games of the Modern
Era in Athens

the partisan Greek spectators.

Greek honour was to be restored by the marathon efforts of farmer Spiridon Louis, who later revealed that while completing his military service a year earlier as groom to the horses of General Mavromichalis, he had been inspired to competition when shown the finish line of the uncompleted Olympic stadium.

To the delight of the 100,000 crowd, the diminutive figure of this Greek athlete emerged through the white marble gates of the Panathenic stadium in first place. Rapturous applause followed as Prince George and Crown Prince Constantine ran to his side urging him to the finish, where an overjoyed King George stood waiting. Louis's time of 2:58:50 was over seven minutes faster than that of second-placed compatriot Charilaos Vasilakos.

It would be another 108 years before the games would return to Athens in their official form, although the enthusiastic Greeks organised an Intercalated (intermediary) Games in 1906. A 1949 commission of the IOC declared that these games were wholly unofficial and the matter has remained closed since.

**BELOW** The start of
the 100 metres sprint
at the first Olympic
Games of the Modern
Era in Athens

# Athens 2004

After leading in all voting rounds, Athens was finally chosen to host the 2004 Olympic Games on 5 September 1997. The Olympics were coming home. An ambitious programme of construction was devised with the intention of constructing state-of-the-art stadiums and, crucially, improving Athens' aging transport infrastructure.

To the watching world it seemed that the Greeks would not finish the project on time as construction appeared shockingly slow. Even by late March 2004, with the Games just five months away, some developments were still behind schedule. The main Olympic stadium was finally completed with just two months to spare.

Controversy struck the Games even before they opened. Greek Olympic 200m champion Kostas Kenderis had been selected to light the Olympic flame at the opening ceremony but, just days before the Games commenced, Kenderis and women's 100 metre silver medallist, Katerina Thanou, missed a random drug test. They subsequently claimed that they had been involved in a motorcycle accident but no record exists of such an accident and neither athlete competed in Athens.

Despite these early setbacks, the Games were a resounding success with 11,099 athletes from 202 countries participating in 301 events across 28 sports.

American Michael Phelps dominated the men's swimming events, collecting six gold and two bronze medals to become only the second man to win eight medals at one Olympic Games. If Phelps were a country he would have come 16th in the medal tables, beating Spain, Canada and New Zealand.

In other waterborne competitions, German canoeist Birgit Fischer became the second athlete in the history of the Games to win

**BELOW** A bronze statue of a discus thrower stands outside the all-marble Panathenaic stadium with the Olympic rings in the background

gold medals at six different Olympics. British yachtsman Ben Ainslie won his second gold medal in the Laser class following his success at Sydney, while compatriot Matthew Pinsent won his fourth consecutive rowing gold medal.

Popular British athlete Kelly Holmes completed an astounding double, taking victory in both the 800 and 1500 metre finals, but the weight of expectation hung heavy around the neck of fellow Briton Paula Radcliffe who, suffering from heat exhaustion and the effects of a stomach bug, was forced to pull out of the women's marathon with just five miles to go.

Moroccan Hicham El Guerrouj achieved an exciting double, winning a gold medal in the 1500 metres and the 5000 metres.

A dramatic men's marathon saw Brazilian Vanderlei de Lima accosted by a spectator while leading the race. Visibly shaken, de Lima was subsequently passed by Italian Stefano Baldini, to finish in third place. For demonstrating fair play, de Lima was awarded the Pierre de Coubertin medal at the closing ceremony.

Having shown promise in Sydney, the British track cycling team made their mark at the Athens Games with Bradley Wiggins collecting three medals, one of each colour, and Scotland's Chris Hoy winning a gold medal in the 1km time trial.

# Atlanta 1996

It seemed a logical, foregone conclusion that the centenary Games would be awarded to Athens, the spiritual home of the Olympics and site of the first modern Games. However, a different logic prevailed. With American corporations providing so much capital investment through rights revenues, the IOC voted in favour of Atlanta by 51 votes to 35.

In spite of some outstanding performances, the 1996 Atlanta Olympics will always be regarded as flawed. Organisation of the Games was extremely poor.

Atlanta's creaking transport infrastructure failed to cope with the demands of the thousands of visiting athletes and spectators, while an outdated computerised results system constantly broke down. Inadequately trained volunteer staff added to the confusion.

There were many complaints of commercial exploitation directed at the Centennial Olympic Park and this location gained further notoriety on July 27 when a bomb exploded, killing one person and injuring 110. Amazingly, the Park had not been included in the Games security system.

In an emotional display, and in the presence of a record 10,310 athletes from 197 nations, the Olympic flame was lit by the frail boxing legend Muhammad Ali who, as Cassius Clay, had won an Olympic light-heavyweight gold medal in 1960.

Carl Lewis of the United States, competing at his fourth Olympics, once again took the gold medal in the long jump to become only the third person to have won the same individual event

**BELOW** Former heavyweight boxing Champion and 1960 OlympIc gold medallist Muhammad Ali lights the flame during the opening ceremony at the Olympic Stadium in Atlanta

on four occasions. In doing so, Lewis took his career tally to nine Olympic gold medals.

With his unique upright action and gold running spikes, America's Michael Johnson became the athletic icon of the games. Johnson, the reigning world record holder over 400m, was last out of the blocks in the Olympic final but quickly recovered, storming into the lead after 300m and pulling away to win by four metres in 43.84 seconds. And in a truly outstanding performance, Johnson demolished his own 200m world record by 0.34 seconds with a time of 19.32 seconds, finishing four metres clear of silver medallist Frankie Fredericks. Timing revealed Johnson had run the last 100m in 9.20 seconds.

French star Marie-José Pérec emulated Johnson's double by taking the 200m and 400m gold medals in the women's events. In taking the 200m/400m double, both Pérec and Johnson had achieved a feat never before seen at the Olympic games in un-boycotted competition.

A more unusual record was broken by Austrian yachtsman Hubert Raudaschl, who became the first competitor to have competed in nine Olympic Games.

**BELOW** An aerial view of the Olympic stadium in Atlanta

# Barcelona 1992

**BELOW** Fireworks during the closing ceremony

In the years between the 1988 Seoul Games and those of Barcelona in 1992, the global map changed almost beyond recognition. The Berlin Wall fell and Germany became once again a unified nation. In South Africa the apartheid system came to an end. Communism collapsed in the Soviet Union, with the territory of the former USSR being split into 15 individual countries.

As Spanish archery Paralympian Antonio Rebollo launched a flaming arrow to light the Olympic flame, the Games of the XXV Olympiad opened with all nations present for the first time in 20 years, with the ex-communist republics competing as the Unified Team. Having taken military action against Croatia and Bosnia-Herzegovina, Yugoslavia was banned from international competition but its individual athletes were given permission to compete as 'Independent Olympic Participants'.

# BARCELONA 1992

**RIGHT** Forward Karl Malone of the United States goes up for two during a game against Germany at the Olympic Games in Barcelona

**BELOW** All around individual gymnast gold medalist Vitaly Scherbo from Unified team (Belarus), shows his gold medal to the public

For the first time, the men's basketball competition was opened to professional athletes. Known as the Dream Team, the United States squad included NBA stars Michael Jordan, Larry Bird, Magic Johnson and Charles Barclay. Averaging 117 points per game, the American team never called a time-out in the entire tournament, defeating Croatia 117-85 to take the gold medal.

The young Belarusian gymnast Vitaly Scherbo had been described by his coach, Aleksandr Arkeyev, as "a showman". Arkeyev's point was to be proved as Scherbo dominated his opposition, winning the parallel bar, long horse vault, rings, pommel horse, team combined and all-round competition to take six gold medals, four of these on a single day. Only the great swimmers Mark Spitz and Michael Phelps have won more gold medals at a single Olympiad.

At 32 years old, Great Britain's Linford Christie achieved a lifetime ambition by beating Namibian Frankie Fredericks and Dennis Mitchell of the United States to become the oldest ever winner of the men's 100m final. The women's 100m final was equally exciting with Gail Devers taking victory despite just six hundredths of a second separating the first five athletes.

On a different kind of track, Britain's Chris Boardman pedalled his way to victory in the 4000m cycling pursuit final. In an event where the result is often determined by hundredths of a second, Boardman achieved the unthinkable and actually lapped his opponent, Jens Lehman. Much hype was centred on Boardman's carbon fibre Lotus-designed cycle, but defeated Lehman insisted he had been beaten by the man and not by the bike.

Popular Italian Fabio Casartelli took victory in the cycling road race. Tragically, Casartelli died of his injuries after crashing on the decent of the Portet-d'Aspet during the 1999 Tour de France.

# Beamon

Forced to train without a coach due to a suspension, 22-year-old Bob Beamon's preparations for the 1968 Mexico City Games were far from ideal. Despite the presence of all three medal winners from the 1964 Tokyo Games, Beamon was considered the favourite having won 22 out of his last 23 meetings.

In the qualification round, Beamon almost ended up with an early plane ticket home as he fouled twice. The 1964 silver medallist, Ralph Boston, suggested that he should make a mark before the take-off board and aim for that, just as Jesse Owens had done in 1936. Beamon qualified easily.

The night before the final, Beamon changed his preparation in a major way. Rather than resting, he chose to go out for a drink and then have sex. He was convinced he had blown his chances.

Seventeen athletes had qualified for the final but the first three fouled, leaving a nervous Beamon to post the first distance of the competition. He sprinted down the runway, hit the board perfectly and glided high through the air. Attempting to calculate his jump, the officials found their special measuring device to be too short. When at last he found out how far he had jumped, Beamon collapsed in shock.

He had jumped an incredible 8.90 metres and set a new world record by 55 centimetres – a record that would last for 22 years 316 days.

**ABOVE** Bob Beamon of the USA breaking the Long Jump World Record during the 1968 Olympic Games in Mexico City

# Beijing 2008

Before Beijing was chosen to host the 2008 Summer Olympic Games, concerns were expressed about China's unproven ability to stage sports events of the Olympics' magnitude, about the country's unenvied reputation in the area of human rights, about the possibility of terrorist attacks, about the city's sweltering heat and levels of pollution. The doubters continued to express their worries right up until the opening ceremony, but when the Games were over most observers agreed they had been an outstanding success.

Beijing had been close to being chosen for the 2000 Games, which ultimately went to Sydney. Having been selected for 2008, the organisers went to town in addressing the critics' concerns and putting on a hell of a show. The athletes – more than 11,000 of them, from 204 countries – showed their gratitude by providing some unforgettable performances.

In total, 37 venues were used during the Olympics, with the equestrian events, staged in Hong Kong, providing a second base. Of those venues, 12 were built especially for the Games, and none was more spectacular than The Bird's Nest. That was the apt nickname given to the inspired design of the new Beijing National Stadium, centrepiece of the Olympics.

The 91,000-capacity stadium hosted the opening and closing ceremonies plus the athletics competition, which held the vast crowds enthralled. They watched open-mouthed as the incomparable Usain Bolt broke two world records in winning gold

medals in the men's 100 and 200 metres. They applauded as world records tumbled in three further events, including the inaugural women's 3000 metre steeplechase. They even showed stoical acceptance as home favourite Liu Xiang, Olympic champion in the 100m hurdles, was forced to withdraw from the competition through injury.

There were outstanding performances in other areas, not least by Chinese athletes, who accounted for 51 of the 302 gold medals on offer. The United States, as usual, topped the medal table with a total of 110, helped in no small degree by the exploits of swimmer Michael Phelps. He left Beijing with eight gold medals in his hand baggage.

Many Olympic and world records were in danger as the Beijing Games approached, and many were duly broken: 43 world and 132 Olympic record were set. One further record was set, and it was a significant one: 86 countries, more than ever before, won at least one medal. Fifty-four countries won at least one gold – another new high.

The Beijing Games were a triumph for two athletes who might normally have been expected to only take part in the Paralympics. South African swimmer Natalie du Toit

became the first amputee to qualify for the Olympics since Oliver Halassy in 1936; and the Polish table tennis player Natalia Partyka, who was born without a right forearm, also competed.

Although criticisms about controls on the media and other issues remained, Beijing was on the whole a tremendous sporting occasion.

**ABOVE** Participators hold the Olympic rings as they take part in a folk dance competition aimed at promoting sporting activities as Beijing gears up to host the 2008 Olympics

# Berlin 1936

**MIDDLE** Aerial view of the Olympic stadium (background) and the Olympic swimming pool

**BELOW** Konrad von Wangenheim with his arm in a sling, shortly before riding 'Kurfurst' in the three day team event

It was clear from the start that the nature of the Berlin Games of 1936 would be like no other. Before the opening, a torch relay had taken place during which a lighted torch was carried from Olympia to Berlin – an institution that lives on to this day. And Adolf Hitler had decided that the Olympics would be an ideal platform from which to demonstrate the racial superiority of the Aryan people. With a well-prepared team of exceptional athletes, 4.5 million tickets sold and the world's press in attendance, it seemed that he might be proved right.

The crack German squad would take 33 gold medals, a vast improvement on the three they collected at Los Angeles in 1932. With images beamed directly on to 28 big screens located about Berlin, the stage was set for Teutonic dominance. But it would be the efforts of African-American athletes Ralph Metcalf, John Woodruff, Cornelius

Johnson and Jesse Owens that would take the headlines of the newspapers and the hearts of devotees the world over.

Sprinter and long jumper Owens finished as the undoubted hero of the Games, taking gold medals in the 100m, 200m, long jump and 4x100m relay. It was reported that, after Owens' victory in the long jump, Hitler refused to offer his congratulations as the athlete did not conform to the Reich Chancellor's view of racial superiority. Owens has since discounted these reports, claiming that he was well treated by the Germans during his stay.

Diminutive Marjorie Gestring from Los Angeles, at just 13 years old, became the youngest ever Olympic gold medallist by taking victory in the women's springboard diving, while Inge Sorrenson, representing Denmark, set another record by becoming the Games' youngest ever individual medallist, taking bronze in the 200 metre breaststroke at the age of just 12.

Incredible personal sacrifice was seen in the actions of Lieutenant Konrad von Wangenheim, a member of the German equestrian three-day event team. A heavy fall in the steeplechase element broke one of von Wangenheim's collarbones but, knowing his failure to finish would result in the disqualification of the German team, he remounted and completed the course.

The following day, this time during the show jumping element, von Wangenheim was again unseated as his horse, Kurfürst, reared and fell upon him. At first onlookers feared he had been killed but he jumped to his feet and remounted to complete the remainder of the course without fault, taking Germany to a much-deserved team gold medal.

# Boardman

The image of Chris Boardman astride his Lotus 'super-bike', powering his way to victory in the 1992 400m individual pursuit, is one of the icons of British Olympic achievement.

Great Britain's cyclists went to Barcelona in the knowledge that their team's last gold medals had been awarded to Harry Ryan and Thomas Lance in 1920. But media attention was drawn to the relatively unknown Boardman after his first round qualification time in the pursuit was posted. Recording 4:27.327, he had taken an astonishing four seconds off the world record time of reigning Olympic champion Gintautas Umaras.

The following evening, Boardman rode his quarter-final against Jan-Bo Petersen of Denmark. Storming home in 4:24.496, he lowered the record by another three seconds despite easing up once he had caught his opponent. In the semi-final, with a win rather than a fast time being important, Boardman eased into a lead over New Zealander Gary Anderson and stayed there to record a relatively slow 4:29.332.

The final pitched Boardman against Germany's world champion, Jens Lehman. Powering smoothly away from the start, Boardman was already in the lead after one lap. Approaching the halfway distance, Lehman's deficit was increased to three seconds, an insurmountable distance to close in a pursuit race. Finally, with one lap remaining, Boardman caught Lehman and secured the gold medal.

With the media giving as much credit to the Lotus bicycle as to Boardman, Lehman graciously insisted he had been beaten by the rider, not the bike.

# Bolt

*"I was slowing down long before the finish and wasn't tired at all. I could have gone back to the start and done it all over again."*

Those were the words Usain Bolt used in his autobiography to describe his astonishing victory in the 100 metres final at the 2008 Beijing Games. The millions who were watching in the stadium and on TV had no reason to disbelieve the Jamican's claim.

Running with one shoelace undone and without the benefit of a following wind, Bolt nevertheless improved on his own world record, finishing in the extraordinary time of 9.69 seconds. It could have been even faster. He was so far ahead of his demoralised opponents by the closing stages that he was able to slow appreciably and indulge in some chest-slapping celebration before crossing the line. Scientists later calculated that Bolt could have chalked up a time of 9.55 if he had not slowed up.

He was accused of showboating and disrespect, but Bolt insisted that wasn't the case and his celebrations were merely the result

**ABOVE** Usain Bolt posing after a victory.

of his happiness at the realisation of his gold medal dream. He was to get a whole lot happier before the Games were over.

By the time the final of the 200 metres came round, the TV audiences had become used to Bolt's playing up to the cameras, his practical jokes and his seemingly relaxed attitude to competition, even on the starting blocks. But his opponents were in no doubt that his playfulness didn't detract one iota from his ability to annihilate the competition. All eyes

were on Michael Johnson's 200 metre world record of 19.32 seconds, which he had set at the 1996 Olympics. Surely Bolt couldn't surpass that great feat?

Oh yes, he could. This time Bolt managed to keep his shoelaces tied and, despite an unhelpful headwind, surged to gold in a new world record time of 19.30 seconds. He thus became the first man to hold the world records for the 100 and 200 metres concurrently since fellow Jamaican Don Quarrie, and the first to break both records at the same Olympic Games.

He wasn't finished with Beijing yet; there was still the 4x100 metre relay to come, and Bolt was set to run the third leg in the final. He duly increased his gold medal count to three as he and the other Jamaican sprinters – Nesta Carter, Michael Frater and Asafa Powell – lowered the Olympic and world records for the event to 37.10 seconds.

There were those who suspected Bolt's miraculous performances in Beijing had more to do with artificial aids than human endeavour, but the runner's coach insisted he could be drug-tested "any time, any day, any part of the body". The golds were due entirely to innate ability, physical gifts and hard work. And as if to prove his humanity, Bolt endeared himself to his Chinese hosts by donating $50,000 to the victims of the 2008 Sichaun earthquake.

# Čáslavská

Czech gymnast Věra Čáslavská was born in Prague in May 1942. Originally a figure skater, she took easily to the grace, balance and physical demands of gymnastics.

A 1958 World Championship team silver medal in her debut international competition gave an indication of the greatness to come, and it was a feat she repeated at her first Olympics, the 1960 Games in Rome.

A second Olympic appearance at the 1964 Games proved to the world what a dominant force the young Czech had become. Gold medals in the individual all-round competition, horse vault and balance beam, plus a silver medal in the team event, made Čáslavská the most successful female gymnast of the Games.

Her fame reached its peak at the 1968 Mexico City Olympics. Two months before the Games, Soviet troops had crossed the border into Czechoslovakia, forcing Čáslavská, an outspoken supporter of the democratic movement, to go into hiding. Granted permission to attend the Games at the last minute, she once again dominated the gymnastics competition, taking gold medals in the individual all-round, floor, asymmetric bars and horse vault, and silver medals for the team all-round and the balance beam.

Čáslavská complemented her gold medals with a gold ring, marrying Czech 1500 metres runner Josef Odložil in a ceremony at the Games. Perhaps inspired by her use of Jarabe Tapatio – the Mexican Hat Dance – for her floor exercise, 10,000 well-wishers attended the wedding.

# Comăneci

**BELOW** Nadia Comaneci celebrating in front of the scoreboard which was unable to display the correct score

It can seem strange that an event as huge as the Olympic Games can be dominated by someone so tiny, but that is exactly what happened at the 1976 Montreal Games when 4 foot 10 inch, 14-year-old Romanian Nadia Comăneci stepped into the limelight.

Born in Onesti in 1961, Comăneci had begun competing in gymnastics at the age of six, representing her hometown. Coached by Bela Karolyi, who later defected to the United States, the young Romanian first came to international prominence at the 1975 European Championships. There she won three gold medals and one silver, beating her idol, the Soviet star Ludmilla Tourischeva.

Initially the media attention in the gymnastic halls of the Montreal Games was focused squarely on the Soviet trio of Tourischeva, Olga Korbut and Nelli Kim. Korbut had just been awarded an outstanding 9.90 in the asymmetric bars when the little Romanian began her routine.

There followed a display of exquisite grace and timing, after which an anxious Comăneci stared at the electronic display, awaiting her score. The score flashed up 1.00. After a brief moment of confusion, the realisation struck home: Comăneci had become the first gymnast to attain 10.0, the perfect score, in Olympic competition. The Swiss Timing scoreboard hadn't foreseen such a result and couldn't display the correct score.

Comăneci went on to score another six 10.0s during the Montreal Games, winning gold medals for individual all-round, balance beam and asymmetric bars, a silver medal in the team all-round and a bronze medal in the floor exercise.

# Combat Sports

Olympic competition includes six forms of combat sport: boxing, freestyle wrestling, Greco-Roman wrestling, judo, taekwondo and fencing.

First introduced at the 1904 St Louis Games, boxing remains the only Olympic sport in which professionals are not allowed to compete, although many, using the Games as a career stepping stone, have gone on to turn professional with great success. They include Cassius Clay, brothers Michael and Leon Spinks, Joe Frazier, George Foreman, Lennox Lewis and Wladimir Klitschko. In recent years, British success has come in the form of Audley Harrison, Amir Khan and James DeGale.

In Olympic competition, boxers fight over three rounds of three minutes in front of a panel of five judges, who electronically score the match depending on the number of blows struck with the white panel of the boxer's glove on the front or sides of his opponent's head or body above the belt. The scoring system is not without controversy.

At the Barcelona 1992 Games, American Eric Griffin was eliminated from the competition after a second round qualification bout against Spaniard Rafael Lozano. Despite comprehensively outscoring his opponent 19-9, 18-9, 26-17, 8-5, 10-9 in the eyes of the judges, he lost the match 5-6 due to the fact that the judges had not pressed their buttons at the same moments in the action. The resulting uproar caused so much embarrassment to the

**ABOVE** Audley Harrison of Great Britain on his way to winning Gold in the Mens 91kg Boxing Final at the 2000 Olympic Games in Sydney, Australia

International Amateur Boxing Association that it has since restricted all access to the scores of individual judges.

Wrestling takes two forms at the Olympic Games. In freestyle wrestling, competitors grapple for two three-minute rounds, scoring technical points for successfully executed holds, manoeuvres, advantage positions and near-throws. A match may be stopped if a wrestler achieves a fall or a ten-point lead.

Greco-Roman wrestling, named in honour of the ancient cultures but actually an invention of 19th century France, uses the same basis of scoring as the freestyle competition but wrestlers are not permitted to use their legs for pushing, pressing, squeezing or lifting an opponent. No hold may be made below the hips.

Judo made its first Olympic appearance as a men's competition at the 1964 Tokyo Games. Women's competition was introduced in 1992. Based upon the unarmed elements of various forms of jujitsu, it was developed in the 1880s by Dr Jigoro Kano who, in 1909, was selected as the first Asian member of the International Olympic Committee.

Olympic judo matches last five minutes for male and four minutes for female judoka. During a match, two judges score each competitor on the moves, holds and throws they execute successfully.

The best moves are declared Ippon, scoring ten points and an instant win. Lesser moves are termed Waza-ari, Yuko or Koka. Two Waza-ari in a match counts as Ippon but any other combination only counts as a cumulative score. An unusual but not altogether surprising rule

for judoka (judo competitors) to observe is that they must be free of unpleasant body odours and possess short fingernails and toenails.

Taekwondo traces its roots back 2,000 years to traditional Korean martial arts, but was actually only invented in 1957. It first appeared in Olympic competition as a demonstration sport in 1988 and again in 1992, receiving recognition as an Olympic sport for men and for women at the Sydney Games in 2000.

Fights are contested over three rounds of three minutes for male competitors and two minutes for females. Competitors attempt to score points by striking defined target areas on their opponent's head and body using the foot below the ankle or the knuckles of the index and middle fingers. All hits below the waist are outlawed.

An Olympic sport since 1896, fencing is one of the few Olympic sports that allowed

the participation of professionals before the 1980s. A fan of the sport, Baron Pierre de Coubertin himself stated unequivocally that fencing 'masters' should be allowed to compete. Women's competitions were introduced to the Olympics at the Paris Games of 1924. Competitions are fought on a 14 metre-long, 1.8 metre-wide piste in three classes, based on the type of weapon used.

The épée has a rigid, heavy blade of triangular cross section with a point covered by a cone, and it may be used to strike the opponent anywhere on the body. The foil is a very light and flexible weapon with a rectangular profile and a blunt point, which may only be used on the trunk of the body, between the collar and the hips. The sabre uses a triangular flexible blade with its point blunted. Both blade and point may be used, but contact is only permitted on the body above the waist, the head and the arms.

All weapons are electronically wired to record hits accurately, lighting up a lamp as they do so.

# Coubertin

Pierre Frédy, later to become Baron de Coubertin, was born on New Year's Day, 1863, to rich, aristocratic, devoutly Catholic parents. His father was a religious painter of some note while his mother, Marie-Marcelle Gigault de Crisenoy de Mirville, was descended from a long line of French noblemen.

It was expected of de Coubertin that he would follow a nobleman's path in life. Religious orders, law and the military beckoned but, despite his strict upbringing, de Coubertin was something of a free spirit, and he was inspired by the work of Thomas Arnold in the sphere of physical education at Rugby School.

In November 1892, aged just 29, he addressed a meeting of the Union of French Athletic Sports Associations – an organisation he had helped form – at the Sorbonne in Paris. With the words "let us export our rowers, runners and fencers", de Coubertin reinforced his case for "this grandiose and virtuous work: the re-establishment of the Olympic Games". His audience applauded politely and then turned him down.

Undeterred, de Coubertin persisted with realising his dream and in 1894 called a conference of his own. Invited were representatives from 12 countries whom de Coubertin had selected believing they would be sympathetic to his plans. The conference was a great success and a unanimous vote was taken to revive the Olympic Games, with de Coubertin appointed to found an organising committee.

Just four years later, under the direction of Baron Pierre de Coubertin, the Games of the First Olympiad were staged in Athens.

**ABOVE** A portrait of Pierre de Fredi Baron de Coubertin, the Frenchman who revived the Olympic Games.

# Cycling

Cycle racing has appeared at every Olympics since 1896, while women's events were first introduced into competition in 1988, with professionals of both sexes permitted to compete since 1996. There are currently three types of Olympic cycling event: road, track and mountain bike racing.

The road cycling programme includes a road race and an individual time trial. The road race begins with a massed start and is contested over a distance between 210 and 240 kilometres on a road-based circuit of between 12 and 18 kilometres.

In the individual time trial, riders are set off at 60-second intervals to race unaided over a course between 45 and 55 kilometres in length. The winner is the rider who completes the course in the shortest time.

The women's road events take place on the same course as the men's. However, both events are run over shorter distances: approximately 120 kilometres for the road race and between 25 and 35 kilometres for the individual time trial.

The Olympic track cycling schedule consists of a specialised and varied programme

of racing.

The 1000 metres match sprint is a tactical game of nerves culminating in a 70kph dash for the line. The time trial is a race against the clock, with riders competing individually on the track to record the best time from a standing start, for either one kilometre for

men or 500 metres for women.

In the individual and team pursuits, two riders or teams of four riders compete against each other from a standing start on opposite sides of the track. The winner is either the first to cross the line or the one who catches the other before the end of the race. The team sprint is similar to the team pursuit but is contested by squads of three riders over just three laps.

The points race, usually 40 kilometres in length, is fast and frantic as riders sprint for points every two kilometres. The race finishes when a rider completes the full distance, with victory being awarded to the rider with the most points who has not been lapped by the first finisher. The Madison is similar to the points race but is contested by teams of two who take turns in riding for points.

Atlanta 1996 heralded the introduction of mountain bike racing into the Olympics. The cross country, held over 40 to 50 kilometres for men and 30 to 40 kilometres for women, is run on dirt tracks and gravel roads with no more than 15 per cent of the course crossing tarmac.

BMX racing made its debut as a full Olympic event at the 2008 Beijing, with the hope that this fast-moving action will stimulate a young audience and encourage participation by countries not normally considered cycling nations.

**ABOVE** Action in the women's mountain bike cross country event during the Athens 2004 Olympic Games

# Discontinued Events

While many events have stood the Olympic test of time, others have, for various reasons, not found their way into the modern Games.

The 1900 Paris Games saw Great Britain – in the form of the touring Devon and Somerset Wanderers XI – take a cricket gold medal after knocking up 262 and defeating a French team consisting almost entirely of British staff from the Paris embassy, who could muster just 104 runs.

A nail-biting competition ensued for glory in the Olympic croquet competition, which resulted in France coming first, second and third overall. The result was influenced somewhat by the fact that no other nation had participated.

Lacrosse made an interesting appearance at the 1904 St Louis Games, with one of the two Canadian teams consisting exclusively of Mohawk players, including Black Eagle, Red Jacket, Almighty Voice, Flat Iron and Man Afraid Soap. The 1908 London Olympics featured motor-boating, the only time a motor-powered sport has featured at the Games.

Pelota Basque, a highly physical ball game

played with a bat or racquet against a wall, featured at the 1900 Paris Games and has since made reappearances as a demonstration sport at both the 1968 and 1992 Olympics. Jeu de Paume, also known as real tennis, made a single appearance at the 1908 Games.

The 1900 Games included some unusual and dramatic variations of equestrian sports including the high jump, long jump and four-in-hand mail coach. In 1920, figure riding was added to the programme. Open to army officers only, this event included jumping on and off a horse, standing on a horse and even jumping over horses.

Fighting broke out at the 1924 Games in Paris as 40,000 passionate French fans looked on in dismay at the last Olympic rugby match to be held. Their fancied team was defeated 17-3 by the unfavoured United States.

American rugby player Daniel Carroll made history, winning a gold medal at the 1920 Antwerp Games having already won Olympic gold 12 years earlier as a member of the conquering Australian team.

Tug of war was a popular event until its discontinuation after the 1920 Antwerp Games. After being pulled over in the first round of the 1908 Games by Great Britain, the American team lodged a protest that their opponents were wearing illegal boots. The protest was disallowed after it was pointed out that the team consisted of members of the Liverpool police and they were wearing standard issue police boots.

# Drugs

There are few sporting competitions that have not at some point been tainted by the use of performance-enhancing drugs. The Olympic Games is no exception, and even its formative years had their share of incidents.

During the marathon event at the 1900 St Louis Olympics, a suffering Thomas Hicks of the United States was administered a cocktail of strychnine and brandy by his helpers. Hicks struggled on to finish and take the gold medal, but he had lost almost five kilograms in body weight during the three and a half hours he had spent running.

Matters came to a head during the road race at the 1960 Rome Games, when Danish cyclist Knut Jensen collapsed and died after consuming a combination of amphetamines and nicotinyl tartrate.

It may be surprising to learn that control over the use of performance-enhancing substances was not introduced by the Medical Commission of the International Olympic Committee until 1967. Unfortunate Swedish modern pentathlete Hans-Gunnar Liljenwall became the first athlete to fall foul of the new regulations during the Mexico City Games of the following year. Anxious prior to the shooting phase of the competition, he had drunk two beers to calm his nerves and subsequently tested positive for alcohol.

Mandatory drug testing was introduced at the 1972 Munich Olympics, but already the doctors and coaches involved in administering performance-enhancing drugs were ahead of the Medical Commission. New substances were formulated and masking agents were developed that tests were unable to detect.

An incredible example of doping en masse existed within the East German Olympic team between 1968 and 1989. The German authorities, convinced that the Olympics were a great weapon of Cold War propaganda, started experimenting with the use of steroids and testosterone. Despite their banned status, by 1978 East German athletes in all sports were being administered anabolic steroids, in many cases without their own knowledge.

For many years, positive tests in Olympic competition were, in the main, given by weightlifters and athletes of a lesser public profile. This changed at the 1988 Seoul Games when Canadian 100 metres winner Ben Johnson was stripped of his gold medal and world record after testing positive for stanozolol. For the first time, a major athlete and hero of the games had been caught cheating.

Drugs continue to be an issue in Olympic sport, with substances being added to the banned list on a regular basis. Unfortunately, with the pressures on athletes to perform and the huge sums of money involved in professional sponsorship deals, it seems inevitable that unscrupulous doctors and trainers will always strive to stay one step ahead of the testing authorities.

**ABOVE** Ben Johnson crosses the finish line to win the Olympic 100 metre final in a world record 9.79 at the 1988 Olympics. Johnson was later disqualified for failing to pass a drug test

# Equestrian

**RIGHT** German dressage rider Ulla Salzgeber rides on her horse at Markopoulo Olympic Equestrian Centre during the final of the individual dressage competition in Athens, 2004

The first appearance of an equestrian event on a modern Olympic programme took place at the Paris Games of 1900 in the form of a show-jumping competition. The 1900 Games also included equestrian high and long jumps and a mail coach driving competition. Nowadays, three equestrian sports are contested at the Games for both individual and team medals: show jumping, dressage and the three-day event.

In the show jumping competition, each horse and rider is required to complete two rounds over a course. The first course of approximately 700 metres in length consists of 12 to 15 jumps varying between 1.4 metres and 1.6 metres in height and including a water obstacle. The second course of ten jumps must differ from the first and be no longer than 600 metres.

Points, known as faults, are awarded should a horse refuse a jump or knock over a pole on a fence. Additional points are awarded if either the horse or its rider fall or if the time limit for the course is exceeded. The winner is the rider/horse combination with the least number of faults. Should there be a tie for first place then a jump-off using several elements of the second course decides the outcome.

The objective of dressage is to express the

responsiveness of a horse to its rider's commands. A series of complex, predefined manoeuvres in all equine paces – walk, trot and canter – are performed in the presence of a panel of judges.

Horse and rider are marked on how well they perform each manoeuvre, the regularity of the paces, the impulsion of the horse, the submissiveness of the horse and the form and position of the rider. In Olympic competition, the top third of the field after an initial test go forward to a second round, from which the best 15 riders advance to the final, a freestyle round performed to music.

The three-day event combines the disciplines of dressage and show jumping, with each horse also required to complete a gruelling cross country course.

The sport of eventing was originally derived from the exercises devised to test the suitability of horses for the military. Until recently, the cross country phase was part of a wider ranging endurance section in which competitors were also required to perform two road-and-tracks courses and a steeplechase, but these have now been dropped in favour of the preferred short-course format.

**ABOVE LEFT** Jeanette Brakewell of Great Britain competes in the eventing cross country competition during the Athens 2004 Olympic Games

**ABOVE** An obstacle in the individual three day eventing jumping final competition during the Athens 2004 Olympic Games

# Ewry

American Ray Ewry must be considered one of the greatest Olympians of all time, but his legend remains almost unknown because the three events at which he excelled are no longer part of the Games.

Born in Lafayette, Indiana in 1873, Ewry contracted polio at an early age and spent much of his youth confined to a wheelchair.

Determined to beat his affliction, the young Ewry started to exercise. As his confidence grew, so did his strength.

Perseverance paid dividends as Ewry not only regained the use of both of his legs but developed into an outstanding athlete specialising in standing jumps.

Competing at the 1900 Paris Olympics, he gained notoriety as "the human frog" by winning gold medals for the standing high jump, standing long jump, at which he set a new world record, and the standing triple jump.

Another Olympics, another moniker. Dubbed "the rubber man" by the American public, Ewry repeated his three-way clean sweep at the 1904 St Louis Games, this time taking the world record for the standing long jump with a distance of 3.47 metres.

With the standing triple jump eliminated from Olympic competition, Ewry was only able to enter two events at the 1908 London Olympics. Predictably, he won both, adding another two gold medals to his tally.

Ewry's story is remarkable not only because of his recovery from polio but also because he was the first athlete in Olympic history to win eight gold medals.

# Flo-Jo

Twenty five-year-old Los Angeles-born Florence Griffith burst on the Olympic scene at the 1984 Games. Despite a creditable silver medal in the women's 200 metres, media and public attention was directed at her outrageously long, painted finger nails rather than her athletic ability.

Following the games, athletics took a back seat in Griffith's life. Marrying 1984 Olympic triple jump champion Al Joyner, she worked in a bank, then as a beautician. Returning to competition prior to the 1988 Seoul Games, 200 metre specialist Florence Griffith-Joyner amazed Olympic selectors by running the 100 metres in 10.49 seconds, a new world record.

Dubbed Flo-Jo by the public, Griffith-Joyner soon became one of the stars of Seoul. Easily winning the 100 metres, she went on to win a gold medal in the 200 metres, setting an unbroken world record of 21.34 seconds, a gold medal in the 4x100 metres relay and a silver medal in the 4x400 metres relay. That was the first time she had competed over 400 metres.

The athlete who had returned was very different from the one who had competed at the 1984 Games. Her stature was that of a body-builder, her jaw-line had squared and her voice had deepened. Although Flo-Jo never once tested positive for drugs, the fact that she retired the day before the introduction of mandatory random drug testing fuelled speculation.

In September 1998, Florence Griffith-Joyner died in her sleep, aged 38.

**ABOVE** Florence Griffith Joyner walks with the American Flag as she celebrates setting a new Olympic record to win the gold medal in the Women's 100 metres final during the 1988 Olympic Games in Seoul

# Fraser

**BELOW** Australian swimming Champion Dawn Fraser (C-without cap) dives for victory in the Olympic ladies 100m free style in October 1964 in Tokyo

Australian Dawn Fraser was taught to swim at the age of five by her brother Donald. A natural in the water, she began competing when she was 11 and was spotted by coach Harry Gallagher at the age of 12.

Fraser's first taste of international competition was the 1956 Melbourne Olympics. Competing in the 100 metres freestyle final, she and compatriot Lorraine Crapp pulled away from the field, with Fraser taking the gold medal and setting a new world record. Success continued with a gold medal in the 4x100 metres freestyle relay and a silver in the 400 metres freestyle.

Undefeated, Fraser arrived in Rome for the 1960 Games and successfully defended her 100 metres freestyle title. The following day, having stayed up late celebrating, Fraser argued with Australian officials, refusing to swim a heat of the medley relay. Despite these problems, Fraser still managed to win two more silver medals, in the 4x100 metres freestyle and medley relays.

Disaster struck during preparation for the 1964 Tokyo Olympics when her car crashed into a truck, killing her mother and leaving Fraser in a neck brace. Remarkably, Fraser recovered in time for the Games where, undeterred, she successfully defended her 100 metres freestyle crown and took silver in the 4x100 metres freestyle relay.

Fraser's career ended after she was arrested for shinning up a flagpole at Emperor Hirohito's palace to collect a souvenir. The charges were dropped and Hirohito gave Fraser the flag as a present, but the antics were too much for the Australian Swimming Union, which issued a ten-year ban for her indiscretion.

# Gebrselassie

Many athletes have won more medals than Haile Gebrselassie, but few have provided such exciting races.

One of ten children, Gebrselassie was born on a farm outside the Ethiopian village of Assela from which, every day, he ran the 20 kilometres to school and back with his books tucked under his arm.

Gebrselassie arrived at the 1996 Atlanta Games as favourite for the 10,000 metres title, although competition was expected from Kenyan Paul Tergat. In the final, Tergat pulled away after 8,000 metres, closely stalked by the Ethiopian. With one lap to go, Gebrselassie pulled alongside and looked at his rival, then sprinted away to win the gold medal.

As the world record holder and undefeated in a 10,000 metres final in seven years, many expected Gebrselassie to be favourite for the 2000 Sydney Olympics, even if his preparations were disrupted by a tendon injury.

In a race always regarded as one of the greatest in Olympic history, Gebrselassie spent time closely tracking the leader and controlling the pace. With seven laps remaining, Kenyan John Korir attacked, reducing the field to seven contenders including Gebrselassie and Tergat. Boxed in with only one lap to go, Tergat pounced at the 250-metre mark. Gebrselassie fought back, pulling alongside the Kenyan with just 50 metres to go. The two battled side by side to the line, where Gebrselassie dipped forward to take victory by 0.09 seconds.

Returning to the Olympics in 2004 with the intention of becoming the first man in history to win three consecutive gold medals in the 10,000 metres, Gebrselassie, hampered by another tendon injury, could only achieve fifth behind compatriot Kenenisa Bekele. In the 2008 Beijing Games, he finished sixth, at the age of 35.

**ABOVE** Haile Gebrselassie of Ethiopia speeds over the track to win the Olympic men's 10,000m gold medal in the Sydney Olympic Games, 2000

# Gymnastics

RIGHT Russian
gymnast Alina
Kavaeva performs
with a rope during
the women's
individual all-around
final for Rhythmic
Gymnastics

Gymnastics were first seen at the Olympics during the inaugural Games of 1896, at which time the events contested included rope climbing and club swinging. Women's gymnastics were introduced as a team event in 1928, with individual competition not being established until the Helsinki Games of 1952.

Competition is split into artistic and rhythmic disciplines. The artistic events comprise three stages – a team competition, an individual all-round competition and individual apparatus finals.

A gymnast from a nation unable to send a full team must still compete in the team competition as it is used as individual qualification. Each nation enters a team of six gymnasts who perform on each of the apparatus – horizontal bar, parallel bars, long horse vault, pommel horse, rings and floor in the case of male competitors and vault, asymmetric bars, balance beam and floor for females.

Following a qualification round, the best eight teams progress to the team final. Two judges assess the difficulty of the routine while a further six mark every competitor out of ten for each exercise. The highest and lowest mark is discarded with the remaining two averaged to give the score. The team event is scored by taking the best of a nation's results across all the apparatus and adding them together to give a team total.

The 36 highest-scoring individual gymnasts from the team competition advance to an individual all-round final, although a maximum of three from each nation is permitted. From this competition, the eight best-performing competitors on each apparatus progress to the individual apparatus finals, although only two gymnasts per nation may compete on any given apparatus.

Trampoline was added to the Olympic programme at the 2000 Games in Sydney, with competitions for men and women. A qualification event comprising compulsory and optional routines is followed by a final contested by the top eight competitors. In this, they are required to perform ten optional moves judged for difficulty and execution.

Rhythmic gymnastics were introduced into the Olympics Games for the first time in 1984 and take the form of an all-round competition.

Competitors perform a musically accompanied freestyle routine in a 12 metre square area using each of four apparatus, which are chosen for each Olympic competition from five available options – hoop, ribbon, ball, rope and club. These apparatus may be in any colour with the exception of gold, silver and bronze.

A gymnast's routine is judged for composition and execution by a panel of judges.

**ABOVE** Dimosthenis Tampakos of Greece, gold medalist on the rings, performs during the Athens 2004 Olympic Games

# Helsinki 1952

**RIGHT** Finnish
runner Nurmi, a
former gold medalist,
lighting the Olympic
flame at the opening
ceremonies for the
Olympics in Helsinki

For the organisers at least, the 1952 Helsinki Olympic Games were to pose a number of difficult questions. Eastern Bloc participation was considered essential if an international spirit were to be maintained, but the host nation had suffered terribly following the Soviet invasion of 1939.

A strong Soviet team did attend, however, and they took home with them a total of 71 medals, 22 of them gold. Russian Aleksandra Chudina showed her athletic versatility by winning silver medals in the long jump and javelin and a bronze medal in the high jump.

Germany, banned from the 1948 Olympics but no longer considered an aggressor, returned to competition in the Games. However, as it had become a divided nation, only athletes from the Federal Republic competed. Japan also made its first appearance since the 1936 Games.

Having previously won a 10,000 metres gold and silver in the 5,000 metres at the 1948 London Olympics, Czechoslovakian long distance runner Emile Zátopek, through a series of outstanding achievements, stole the 1952 Games. Four days after successfully defending his 10,000 metres title, he took the 5,000 metres gold that had eluded him four years previously.

Later in the same week, Zátopek sprinted to victory in the marathon, winning by an incredible two-minute margin. Amazingly, it was the first time he had ever competed in a marathon.

# Holmes

There cannot be many photographs of athletic achievement more memorable than those that capture the elation of Kelly Holmes as she crosses the finishing line of the 800 and 1500 metres at Athens 2004 in gold medal position. Her expression tells of pure joy, surprise, relief, even shock … and it tells of a life's dream come true.

Holmes joined her local athletics club when she was 12 and was an English schools champion by the time she was 13, but a career in the army took her away from the track for a while. While watching Sebastian Coe win gold in the Moscow Olympics 1500 metres she became inspired to emulate her hero, and the discipline of army life stood her in good stead when she returned to athletic competition at the age of 22.

The road to Olympic glory, although waymarked by considerable success, was long and hard, and the year leading up to Athens saw injury and crippling depression threaten to deprive Holmes of her dream. It was not until shortly before the Games that she decided to run the 800 as well as the 1500. It was a good decision.

The final of the 800 saw Holmes, showing impeccable tactical awareness, overhauling Mozambique's Maria Mutola in the final straight. In the 1500 metres she came from the back of the field once again to close out Tatyana Tomashova of Russia and record a new British record time of 3:57.90. She had become the first Briton to win two gold medals at the same Games since Albert Hill in 1920.

**BELOW** Kelly Holmes at one of the many awards ceremonies she has attended.

# How Many?

A spectator at one of the 21st century's Olympic Games events would have difficulty recognising those of the late 19th century. The inaugural Athens Games of 1896 were a small affair when compared to the leviathan that is the modern Olympics.

With only nine sports on the programme – track and field, cycling, fencing, gymnastics, wrestling, weightlifting, shooting, swimming and tennis – just 43 medal events were contested by a total of 245 athletes, all of whom were male, in the presence of an estimated 80,000 spectators. Of the 14 nations represented, 11 were from Europe, with the exceptions being the United States, Chile and Egypt.

By the time the Games reached the People's Republic of China in 2008 – 112 years later – they had grown beyond comparison. Competitors from no fewer than 204 National Olympic Committees vied for the medals spread across 28 sports, and 87 nations returned home with at least one medal. Medals were contested in 302 events in sports that now included the likes of triathlon, beach volleyball, taekwondo and BMX. A total of 10,942 athletes, of whom 4,637 were women, competed in Beijing, from countries as far afield as Burkina Faso and Kiribati.

Seventy thousand volunteers ensured the Games ran smoothly, and 159 countries were represented among the 24,562 accredited media personnel. It's thought that, worldwide, 4.7 billion viewers caught at least some of the Beijing action on their TVs.

**RIGHT** A statue promoting Beijing"s bid to host the 2008 Olympic Games

# Hoy

If things had turned out differently, Chris Hoy might have challenged for Olympic medals in any one of a number of sports. He showed some early promise on the rugby field and rowed for Scotland as a junior, but it was on two wheels that he has truly shone.

It's said the film ET the Extra-Terrestrial inspired Hoy to take to a bicycle at the age of six, and he was soon making an impression in the world of BMX. He competed in that discipline until he was 14, becoming champion of Scotland and ranking number nine in the world.

But it is in indoor sprint cycling that he has left an indelible mark on the Olympics. Hoy started to compete in track sprint cycling in 1994, and was soon picking up medals in world championship events. In 2000, in the Sydney Olympic Games, he was part of the British trio, with Craig Maclean and Jason Queally, that took silver in the men's team sprint behind France.

It was an auspicious Olympic debut but four years later, in Athens, Hoy went one better. The Olympic record was broken four times during that summer's one kilometre time trial, and it was Hoy who set the final record as he dealt with the challenge of Arnaud Tournant of France and Germany's Stefan Nimke in taking the gold medal with a time of 1:00.711.

Hoy had ensured the time trial honours stayed with Britain – Queally had won in Sydney in 2000 – but the event was dropped

**ABOVE** Gold medalist Chris Hoy after his win

**ABOVE** Chris Hoy with fellow Team GB gold medalist Rebecca Adlington

from the programme for the 2008 Beijing Games. Undeterred, he moved his attention to other events – the individual sprint, the team sprint and the Keirin – in a move that was to pay huge rewards. The 2008 Olympics were massively successful for British cyclists but Hoy's contribution was outstanding.

First, in the team sprint on August 15, the British team consisting of Hoy, Jason Kenny and Jamie Staff clocked a world record time

of 42.950 as they saw off France in the gold medal match. Then, a day later, Hoy claimed victory in the Keirin ahead of compatriot Ross Edgar. Finally, on August 19, he beat his teammate Kenny in the individual sprint to get his hands on his third gold medal of the Games.

Not only had Hoy become the most successful Scottish Olympic competitor of all time, he had gone down in the record books as the most successful male cyclist in the history of the Games. In addition, he had become the first British athlete to claim three gold medals in a single Games since the swimmer Henry Taylor in 1908.

Not surprisingly, Hoy was knighted in recognition of his achievements in 2009, and he is to represent Great Britain as an ambassador of the 2012 Olympics in London.

# IOC

The International Olympic Committee was formed by Baron Pierre de Coubertin on 23 June 1894 with the task of reinstating the Olympic Games in a modern form. The IOC has continued its work and is now responsible for the administration of all Olympics-related matters under the watchful eye of its president, Jacques Rogge, who is due to leave office in 2013.

The 115 members of the committee were originally co-opted, with royalty and members of the aristocracy being favoured. However, in recent years there has been a drive towards the allocation of seats to athletes and leaders of international and national federations, in an attempt to represent the world of sport more fully.

Every four years, an executive board of the IOC chooses five locations as candidate cities from a list of applicants, based on their responses to a standard questionnaire. The committee members are then responsible for voting on which city is to be awarded the summer and winter Olympics.

The IOC has in recent years been implicated in a number of scandals involving unscrupulous committee members taking advantage of their position to gain favours from candidate cities, and has been forced to take action to clean up its tarnished image.

**ABOVE** Members of the International Olympic Committee during the 1896 Olympic Games in Athens, Greece.

# Johnson

**RIGHT** Michael
Johnson celebrates
after he set a new
world record time of
19.32 seconds in the
Olympic 200m race
in Atlanta

Michael Johnson, one of the greatest athletes ever to grace the Olympic Games, had a unique running style, with head bobbing upright, that earned him the nickname 'The Duck'.

When Johnson was asked, "If you had a usual running technique like other runners, do you think you would go faster?" he responded, "If I ran like all the other runners, I would be back there with them."

His first Olympic appearance was at Barcelona in 1992. Ranked world number one, the Texan was expected to take the 200 metres title but, 12 days before the Games, he contracted food poisoning. Weakened, he was eliminated in the semi-finals, allowing compatriot Michael Marsh to take the gold. As consolation, Johnson collected a gold medal as part of the victorious US 4x400 metres relay team.

He made amends in Atlanta. Competing in gold running shoes, he won the 400 metres final by over a second from Britain's Roger Black then, in the 200 metres final, he made history. Recovering after a poor start, Johnson powered through the bend until, with 90 metres to go, he went into light-speed to win by four metres, demolishing his own world record by 0.34 seconds. He had run the last 100 metres in 9.20 seconds.

Missing out on 200 metres selection due to injury, Johnson headed to the Sydney with the 400 metres in his sights once more. In the final he was again the slowest to start but with 100 metres remaining he pulled away to win by four metres and become the first man to win twice at the distance. To finish a perfect career Johnson again won a gold medal in the 4x400 metres relay.

# Kayaks and Canoes

Canoeing has been part of the Olympics since the Berlin Games of 1936, and events for women have been included since 1948. The canoeing events are split into two types – kayaks and Canadians.

Kayaks, which are derived from the craft of the Inuit tribes, have a pointed bow and stern and a closed-in deck. The competitor sits within the craft with their legs stretched forward, and uses a long, double-ended paddle to propel the kayak forward. In flat-water races, the kayak makes use of a small rudder to trim its course.

Canadian canoes, developed from those of the native North Americans, bring the competitor into a kneeling position and feature either an open deck for flat-water races or a closed deck for slaloms. The paddle used in this type is shorter and single bladed, and it is switched from side to side to control and propel the canoe.

Separate flat-water competitions are held for both kayaks and Canadians over 500 and 1,000 metres and are contested by individuals and pairs. A 1,000 metres flat-water event is also held for team of four using special kayaks over 11 metres long.

Slalom events require the competitor to paddle down a fast-flowing course while negotiating their way through 25 gates, six of which must be upstream. Penalty points are incurred if a competitor touches a gate, and the winner is the canoeist with the best combined time and penalty score.

**BELOW** Miss Richards an 1948 Olympic contender.

# Korbut

**BELOW** Olga Korbut performs on the beam during the Olympic Gymnastics individual event in Munich where she captured four gold medals

Gymnast Olga Korbut was born in the Belarusian city of Grodno in 1955. Known as the Sparrow of Minsk, she took up gymnastics at the age of eight and entered a training school aged 11, under the guidance of Renald Knysh.

Competing at her first Olympic Games in 1972, the tiny 17-year-old captured the hearts of the Munich crowds and wowed the television audience with an outstanding asymmetric bar performance in the team event. Finishing third athlete overall in the team competition, Korbut appeared capable of causing an upset in the individual competition.

Two days later, the individual all-round final started. To the delight of the crowds and media, Korbut moved into the lead at the halfway point.

The asymmetric bars on which she had performed so well in the team competition were next. Disaster struck. Mounting the bars, she scuffed the mat then, during the routine, she fell from the bars and missed a simple manoeuvre. Unable to hide her disappointment she returned to the bench and wept as the judges awarded her a lowly 7.50.

The next day, in the individual apparatus finals, her form returned. With the world watching on television, she won a silver medal on the asymmetric bars and then gold medals for the balance beam and the floor exercise.

Korbut's subsequent fame was such that back home in Grodno the post office had to employ a special clerk to sort the 20,000 fan letters she received each year.

# Latynina

The gymnast Larisa Latynina holds the record for the most outstanding overall achievement by an Olympic athlete.

Growing up in the Ukrainian town of Kherson, she took to ballet at an early age, only turning to gymnastics after her instructor moved away. At 19 she first competed internationally, winning a team gold medal at the 1954 World Championships.

Her Olympic debut came at the 1956 Melbourne Games. The young Latynina fought hard against the more experienced Hungarian Agnes Keleti to take gold medals in the individual and team all-round competitions. To this she added gold medals on the floor and vault, a silver medal on the asymmetric bars and a bronze medal in the now discontinued portable apparatus event.

Latynina arrived in Rome for the 1960 Games as the clear favourite. Winning the individual all-round competition for a second time, she then led the Soviets to a decisive win in the team competition. Successfully defending her floor title, she then took silver medals for the balance beam and asymmetric bars and a bronze medal in the vault.

Returning for her third Games at the 1964 Tokyo Olympics, Latynina won gold medals in the floor event and for the all-round team but was finally defeated in the all-round competition by Czech Věra Cáslavská, securing only a silver medal. A silver in the vault and bronze for the asymmetric bars and balance beam added to her medal tally.

Latynina finished her Olympic career the holder of 18 Olympic medals – nine gold, five silver and four bronze – and remains to this day the Games' most prolific medal winner.

**ABOVE** Larissa Latynina performs her routine on the beam during the Olympic Games in Melbourne, 1956

# London 1908

Following the eruption of Mount Vesuvius in April 1906, the Italian government, considering its resources would be best placed elsewhere, requested that the 1908 Olympics, planned for Rome, be moved. The IOC obliged, relocating the games to London, and a new stadium with running track, swimming pool, cycling track and football pitch was hastily constructed in Shepherd's Bush.

At the opening ceremony, in the presence of King Edward VII, athletes marched into the stadium in national teams behind their national flag for the first time, a tradition that has been upheld ever since.

Willy and Lottie Dod, representing Great Britain, became the first brother and sister medallists, collecting gold and silver in the archery. Swede Oscar Swahn, at the age of 60, became the Olympic Games' oldest gold medallist, outshooting 14 rivals to win the single-shot running deer competition.

America's Ray Ewry won the standing high jump and standing long jump competitions for the third time and became the only person to win a career total of eight individual Olympic gold medals.

Italian Dorando Pietri captured the hearts of the public in a dramatic finale to the marathon. On entering the stadium after 26 miles, Pietri collapsed five times before being helped across the finishing line by officials. Sadly, he was subsequently disqualified for receiving external assistance.

# London 1948

The 1940 Games, awarded to Tokyo, were hastily reallocated to Helsinki following Japan's invasion of China, but the winds of change were blowing over a much wider area. The subsequent Soviet invasion of Finland and the encroaching prospect of a war in Europe saw the 1940 Games and the planned 1944 London Olympics cancelled all together.

The task of organising the first post-war Olympic Games was never going to be an easy one but, with typical resolve, it was the British Olympic Committee that stepped in to fill the breech.

There would be three notable absences from the 1948 Games: Germany, which was banned from competition and not invited; Japan, which although invited declined to attend; and the Soviet Union, which was in a state of sporting and political isolation. Incredibly however, 59 nations were still represented with more than 4,000 athletes taking part.

In many cases facilities were Spartan – athletes were accommodated in army barracks – but there was a taste of the Games to come as, for the first time, television cameras were

present, with events being broadcast to an expectant nation.

Czechoslovakian canoeist Jan Brzák and Hungarian fencer Ilona Elek surprised many when they both retained the titles they had won at the 1936 Berlin Olympics. At one point in her competition, Elek had trailed American Maria Cerra 2-0, but a remarkable four successive hits took her through to a final bout against Denmark's Karen Lachmann, which she won 4-2 to take the gold.

But the undoubted star of the Games was the 30-year-old Fanny Blankers-Koen of Holland. A world record holder in six disciplines, Blankers-Koen was restricted by an

**ABOVE** Richard Burnell and Bertram Bushnell of Great Britain near the finish at Henley-on-Thames, soon to become the winners in the Double Sculls Final

**ABOVE** A BBC camera films the proceedings at Wembley Stadium as King George VI takes the March Past 6,000 athletes representing 58 countries, at the Opening Ceremony of the 1948 Olympics

**ABOVE RIGHT** British athlete John Mark lights the Olympic Flame at the opening ceremony

Olympic regulation that permitted an athlete to enter only four events. Choosing to compete in the 100m, 200m, 80m hurdles and the 4x100m relay, she hammered home her dominance and returned home with four gold medals.

Audrey Patterson of the United States made Olympic history by taking third place behind Blankers-Koen in the 200m and becoming the first black female athlete to win an Olympic medal. Her compatriot Alice Coachman would, the next day, take victory in the women's high jump to become the first black female gold medallist.

But perhaps the most amazing achievement of the Games was that of Hungarian pistol shooter Karoly Takács. A member of the 1938 World Championship-winning team, Takács had lost his shooting hand to a grenade during the war. Undeterred, he taught himself to shoot left-handed and went on to earn himself an Olympic gold medal in the rapid-fire pistol shoot.

# Los Angeles 1932

The Great Depression even left its unwelcome mark upon the Olympics. With millions unemployed worldwide following the 1929 Wall Street crash, and the sinister rise of extremist attitudes in parts of Europe, a mere 1,503 athletes attended the Los Angeles Games of 1932.

Despite these difficulties, the Games were far from a failure. Record crowds, including many Hollywood celebrities, flocked to the games; the Opening Ceremony at the LA Coliseum attracted 100,000 spectators. Incredibly, considering the prevailing economic climate, the 1932 Olympics were the first Games to turn a profit.

And there were other firsts in Los Angeles. The three-tiered victory rostrum was introduced, as was the protocol of raising the national flag of a victorious competitor.

Electronic timing and photo finishes were included officially (having made their unofficial debut at the 1912 Games) and for the first time a medal result was changed after a photo finish review. A true sportsman,

American Jack Keller, who had incorrectly been awarded a bronze medal in the 110m hurdles, tracked down Briton Donald Finley to personally hand over his medal.

Despite the fact that she qualified for five track and field events, Olympic rules prevented American Mildred 'Babe' Didrikson from competing in more than three. But world records in the high jump and 80m hurdles and victory in the javelin assured her of a place in Olympic history.

**ABOVE** Mildred Didrikson of the USA throws the javelin to win the gold medal

# Los Angeles 1984

**RIGHT** Joan Benoit does a victory lap carrying a US flag after winning the women's marathon

Los Angeles was the only city prepared to bid for the right to host the 1984 Games, other nations having been deterred by the terrorist actions of the Munich Games and the financial debacle of those in Montreal. For the first time since 1896, the Games became dependent on the financial support of corporate sponsorship as significant federal funding was not made available. Unwittingly, these games would set the blueprint for future Olympics.

Unsurprisingly, considering the US-led boycott of the Moscow Games, the Soviet Union declined its invitation to attend, citing anti-communist demonstrations in the USA and a worry for the safety of their athletes as the reason.

Compared to the 65 nations that had rejected their invitations to the 1980 Olympics, only 14 declined to attend the 1984 Games in support of the USSR. This number may seem small but these nations accounted for 58 per cent of the gold medals awarded at the 1976 Montreal Games. In total, a record 140 nations were represented at the 1984 Olympics.

In winning gold medals in the men's 100m, 200m, long jump and the 4x100m relay, 23-year-old American Carl Lewis not only delighted the thoroughly partisan crowd but also matched the 1936 achievement of his hero, Jesse Owens. The 400m hurdles gold medallist in 1976, Edwin Moses, won the event for the second time having missed out in 1980 due to the western boycott.

The Los Angeles games would see a number of Olympic firsts for female athletes. American Joan Benoit won the first women's marathon with her compatriot, Connie Carpenter-Phinney, winning the inaugural

women's cycling road race. Other events to be added included women's rhythmic gymnastics and synchronised swimming.

Controversy surrounded the final of the women's 3000m as barefoot British athlete Zola Budd collided with favourite Mary Decker of the USA, bringing her to the ground. Although it was apparent that Decker was largely at fault,

it was Budd who felt the wrath of the nationalist American public.

West Germany's Ulrike Meyfarth had set a record at the 1972 Games in winning the high jump at the age of 16 and becoming the youngest winner of an individual track and field event. In 1984, she again won that title, becoming the oldest winner of the event – an honour that is now held by Stefka Kostadinova of Bulgaria.

In the rowing, a young and little known Steve Redgrave representing Great Britain won his first Olympic gold medal in the coxless fours, giving spectators a taste of what was to come over the next 16 years.

**ABOVE LEFT** The women's 3,000 metre race with left to right Wendy Sly of Great Britain (silver medal), Zola Budd of Great Britain (gold medal), Maricica Puica of Romania and Mary Decker of the USA

**ABOVE** View of the human Olympic ring formations

# Louganis

Of Swedish/Samoan descent, Greg Louganis was given up by his 15-year-old parents and adopted by a Greek-American family. Constantly bullied by his classmates due to his dyslexia and dark skin, by the age of nine he was smoking tobacco and by 12 he had moved on to marijuana, becoming dependent on alcohol as a teenager. He found his escape in diving.

Qualifying for the 1976 Montreal Olympics at the age of 16, Louganis won a silver medal in the platform dive and finished a respectable sixth in the springboard. Unfortunately, due to the American boycott of the Moscow Games, it was 1984 before he could re-enter the Olympic arena.

Ignoring the pressure of being favourite, Louganis executed a series of outstanding dives, first winning the springboard with an unprecedented 92 points then executing a perfect reverse tuck to take the platform. He had become the first diver to score in excess of 700 points in the event and the first since 1928 to win both medals.

Returning to the Games in 1988, Louganis miscalculated his ninth dive in the springboard preliminaries, cracking the back of his head on the board. With sutures applied he dived once more, attaining the highest score of the day and going on to take the gold medal in the final.

The platform competition was much closer than in 1994. Only by performing a difficult reverse three-somersault in tuck was Louganis able to take gold by the narrowest of margins from 14-year-old Xiong Ni of China.

**RIGHT** Greg Louganis bangs his head against the board after mistiming his dive during the Olympic competition in Seoul

# Mascots

Since its introduction at the 1972 Munich Games, the mascot has become an integral part of the Olympic image. Its purpose is to promote the culture and history of the host city and to convey the spirit of the Games, especially to younger generations.

Waldi, a brightly coloured dachshund, had the honour of being the first Olympic mascot. An instant hit with the public, his qualities of resistance, tenacity and agility were said to mirror those required in an Olympic athlete.

Amik the Beaver was introduced in 1976 at Montreal. The name Amik (meaning beaver, chosen to represent hard work) was taken from the Algonquian language of the Native Americans.

Created by Victor Chizikov, a famous Russian illustrator of children's books, Misha the Bear, mascot for the 1980 Moscow Games, remains the most popular and instantly recognisable Olympic mascot of all time.

Not to be outdone by their eastern adversaries, American organisers enlisted Walt Disney to design Sam the Eagle, mascot of the 1984 Los Angeles Olympics. Resplendent in star-spangled garb, Sam was the first mascot to be thoroughly exploited for commercial purposes, somewhat echoing the feel of the 1984 Games themselves.

Sporting a traditional Korean hat with the Olympic rings suspended from a ribbon around his neck, Hodori the Tiger was designed by Kim Hyun as the mascot for the 1988 Seoul Games. Hodori reflected the hospitable nature of the Korean people. His name was derived from the Korean words Ho (tiger) and Dori, a jovial term for little boys.

**ABOVE** The Athens 2004 summer games official mascots Phevos (L) and Athena Seoul

Cobi the Dog, created by Valencian artist Javier Mariscal, with his smart shirt and tie and beaming smile, was chosen as the mascot of the 1992 Barcelona Games. Cobi starred in his own series on Spanish television.

The first mascot to be designed using computers was Izzy for the 1996 Atlanta Games. The name of this confused character, which was like a being from a video game, came about because nobody seemed to quite know what it was.

Olly, Syd and Millie, their names derived from the words Olympic, Sydney and Millennium, were the first multiple mascots for a Games. Representing generosity, environment and technology, these characters heralded a new chapter in Olympic history.

Based on ancient dolls found in Greece, brother and sister Phevos and Athena were the mascots of the 2004 Athens Games and were named after the Greek god of light and music and the goddess of wisdom.

For the 2008 Beijing Olympics, the Chinese organisers created five mascots. Known collectively as The Friendlies, each had a rhyming two-syllable name, used in China as a term of endearment for children. Beibei the fish was joined by Jingjing the panda, Huanhuan the Olympic flame, Yingying the Tibetan antelope and Nini the swallow. When the names are put together – Bei Jing Huan Ying Ni – they say 'Welcome to Beijing'.

# Medals

It was not until the St Louis Games of 1904 that gold, silver and bronze medals were awarded for first, second and third place. Prior to St Louis, winners would be presented with a silver medal and an olive branch and the runner-up with just a medal. The unfortunate third-placed athlete would get nothing more than the congratulations of officials and his peers.

Over the years some athletes have amassed an amazing tally of medals. Ukrainian gymnast Larissa Latynina boasts the greatest haul, winning a stunning 18 medals, five of which were gold, won between 1956 and 1964. American Michael Phelps holds the overall medal record for men: 16 overall, an amazing 14 of which are gold.

After Phelps, four competitors share the honour of having won the next highest number of Olympic gold medals. Latynina, Paavo Nurmi of Finland and Americans Mark Spitz and Carl Lewis have each won nine golds. Another gymnast, Vitaly Scherbo of Belarus, holds the record for the most gold medals won in a single day, having collected four at the 1992 Barcelona Games.

Having won a gold medal at the 1932 Los Angeles Games, Hungarian fencer Aladár Gerevich astonished crowds by repeating the feat a full 28 years later, at the 1960 Rome Olympics.

**ABOVE** The commemorative medal from the 1904 St Louis Olympic Games

# Melbourne 1956

**RIGHT** Australian athlete Ron Clarke carries the Olympic torch into the stadium during the opening ceremony of the 1956 Olympic games in Melbourne

When, in 1949, the IOC nominated Melbourne as host city for the 1956 Olympic Games, it could have not seen the unusual problem that would come to light.

It was only in 1954 that the implications of Australia's requirement for all horses to spend a six-month period in quarantine were fully appreciated. With the Games at stake, the decision was taken to hold the equestrian events in Stockholm during May – some six months earlier than the events to be held in Melbourne.

Once again, the games were surrounded by political intrigue and controversy. Egypt, Iraq and Lebanon withdrew in protest over the occupation by French and British forces of the Suez Canal and the Israeli incursion into Sinai. Switzerland, Spain and the Netherlands absented themselves in reaction to the Soviet invasion of Hungary. China also boycotted the Games to avoid meeting Taiwan (then known as Formosa). On a more positive note, East and West Germany entered a combined team and were warmly received.

Political tensions overflowed as Hungary, the reigning Olympic water polo champions, were drawn to meet the USSR in a match that would decide the outcome of the gold medal. Just a month earlier, 200,000 Soviet troops had quashed the Budapest uprising.

Though tactically inferior, the Hungarians managed to stamp their authority on the match, playing tight defensive formations and running out exciting and decisive breaks. In the closing minutes, Russian Valentin Prokopov struck out at Hungarian Ervin Zádor, badly splitting

his eyebrow. As blood gushed the fists began to fly, the referee wisely calling the game to a premature halt and declaring Hungary the victors.

Ukrainian Viktor Chukarin and Hungary's Ágnes Keleti dominated the gymnastics. Churakin won five medals, three of them gold, to take his lifetime Olympic medal tally to 11, while Keleti's four gold and two silver medals took her total to ten.

A new discipline was added to the swimming competition as the butterfly stroke was separated from the breaststroke, with American William Yorzyk taking the gold medal. For the first time, a fibreglass pole was used in the pole vault competition (they had previously been used in the 1952 decathlon) and it assisted Georgios Roubanis of Greece to a bronze medal.

With only 15 minutes to go before the weigh-in, bantamweight weightlifter Charles Vinci of the USA found himself to be 200 grams overweight. Only by means of a rather severe military haircut was he able to make the weight and qualify for the competition. Vinci went on to take the gold medal.

# Mexico City 1968

**BELOW** Two athletes fall victim to the high altitudes of the 1968 Olympics in Mexico City

In October 1968, Mexico City hosted the Summer Olympics, with its official name being the 'Games of the XIX Olympiad'. Mexico City made way for many new traditions and customs for future Olympics hosts. Not only was it the first developing country to host the Olympic Games, but they were also the first Spanish speaking country. So far, it is the only games event ever held in Latin America, until 2016 when Rio de Janeiro is due to host the Summer Olympics. This particular games event is remembered for many firsts, including Norma Enriqueta Basilio de Sotelo being the first woman to light the Olympic cauldron with the Olympic flame. Also, it was the first time the closing ceremony of the games were transmitted to the world in colour television.

When Mexico City were selected to host the Olympics, concerns were raised due to the city's high altitude (2,300 m). However, the altitude seemed to be an advantage for athletes competing in explosive events such as jumping, throwing and weightlifting, with many events achieving record-setting scores. The long jump record was beaten by Bob Beamon, who jumped 8.90 m, achieving a 55 cm improvement over the previous world record. This incredible record jump stood until 1991, when it was broken by Mike Powell, who still holds the record to date at 8.95 m. Dick Fosbury won the gold medal in the high jump event, using a radical technique (now named the Fosbury flop).

Al Oerter, an American discus thrower, won his fourth consecutive gold medal in that event and became the first athlete to achieve this feat in track and field and the second in an individual event. Jim Hines and Lee Evans, American athletes, set new world records in

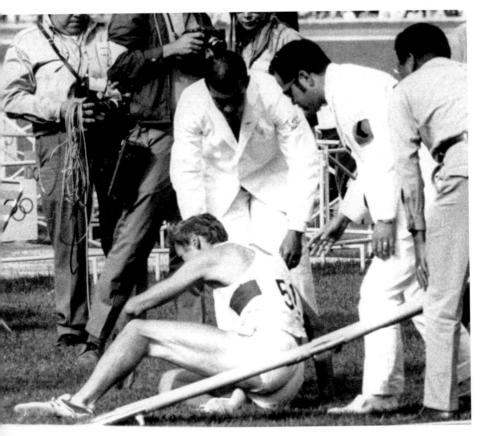

the 100 m and 400 m races, which subsequently stood for many years.

Other triumphs include Debbie Meyer, a 16 year old American swimmer, who became the first swimmer to win three gold medals in the 200 m, 400 m and 800 m freestyle events. Vêra Cáslavská won 4 gold and 2 silver medals in gymnastics and John Stephen Akhwari became internationally famous for finishing last place in the marathon, despite having dislocated his knee.

Along with the high altitude location, there were many other controversies surrounding the games. Prior to the Olympic games starting, North Korea withdrew all of its athletes from Mexico City because the International Olympic Committe refused to refer to the country by its official name, the Democratic People's Republic of Korea.

During the medal presentation ceremony, two African-American athletes, Tommie Smith and John Carlos, made a stand against racism when their country's national anthem was played. They wore a black glove and raised their fists in the air, whilst hanging their heads. They were protesting against racial segregation in the United States, however their actions led to them being expelled from the Olympic Village.

The 1968 Summer Olympics saw many firsts, including many events being timed manually and electronically and the introduction of Doping tests for all winners.

**ABOVE** Balloons being released over the stadium at the opening ceremony of the Olympic Games in Mexico City

# Montreal 1976

**BELOW** Queen
Elizabeth II
opening the 1976
Montreal Olympics

The Montreal Games of 1976 were hit by a wave of political turmoil. Although rugby was not affiliated to the Olympic movement, the fact that the New Zealand All Blacks had recently toured South Africa was seen as an issue.

Hundreds of black South Africans had been shot at a student protest in Soweto, causing Tanzanian president Julius Nyerere to call for New Zealand's exclusion from the games. When the IOC would not capitulate, 27 African nations elected to withdraw.

Under pressure from powerful communist China, the weak-willed Canadian government revoked the visas of the Taiwanese team, who were already resident in the Olympic village. Despite protests from the IOC, the Taiwanese returned home. In reaction to the IOC's stand, the Chinese failed to attend.

Montreal's Olympic project was grand to the extreme but poor financial planning and management, coupled with a series of industrial disputes, saw costs spiral from an estimated $124 million to in excess of $2 billion, the Olympic stadium itself costing $485 million even with its roof unfinished.

Uniquely, the Olympic flame was 'transmitted' by satellite from Athens to Ottawa, where a laser bean was used to light the torch to be carried to Montreal. At the opening ceremony, in the presence of Queen Elizabeth, the Olympic flame was lit by athletes Sandra Henderson and Stéphane Préfontaine.

A few days later a torrential rainstorm doused the flames, resulting in an official relighting the eternal Olympic symbol with his cigarette lighter!

In spite of the absentees from the African nations, the level of competition was high. Of the 26 contested, new world records were set in 21 swimming events and tied in one more.

The split of these medals was clear. In the men's events, 12 of the 13 events were won by American swimmers, while in the women's competition 11 titles went to East Germany. The East German athletes had come from nowhere, and there were suspicions, later confirmed, that they were involved in the use of performance-enhancing drugs.

Nadia Comăneci, a petite 14-year-old Romanian, lit up the games with her gymnastic performances. With her trademark smile in place, she completed an outstanding routine on the asymmetric bars and then stood anxiously watching for her score. It was a 10.0; a perfect score, awarded for the first time in Olympic competition.

Comăneci proceeded to score a further six 10.0s on the way to winning three gold medals, one silver and one bronze.

# Moscow 1980

In December 1979, Soviet troops invaded Afghanistan, provoking anger and condemnation throughout the world. This anger manifested itself in no one more than US president Jimmy Carter.

With an election looming, Carter instigated a campaign to boycott the imminent Moscow Olympics. Global opinion was mixed. Many nations wanted a complete boycott while others wanted to participate. A third group of nations, including Great Britain, France and Spain, wanted to compete without national emblems.

The games opened on 19 July 1980, the Olympic flame being lit by Russian basketball star Serge Belov. There was no coincidence in the choosing of Belov as it was he who had scored the controversial winning point in the 1976 final against the undefeated USA team.

Only 81 nations were represented, the lowest number since the Melbourne Games of 1956, but the quality of performance was exceptionally high as 34 world records and 62 Olympic records were broken.

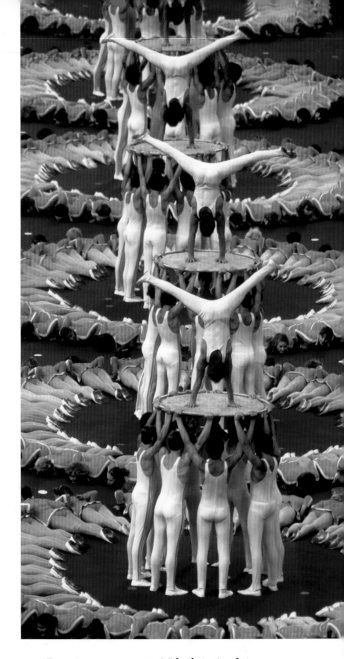

Russian gymnast Nikolai Andrianov won five medals, taking his career total to 15 medals and seven golds. This astounding feat was soon eclipsed by compatriot Aleksandr Dityatin who, by winning a medal in every men's gymnastic event, became the only athlete in history to win eight medals at one Olympics.

Building on their success in Montreal, the East German women's swimming team dominated in the pool, winning 11 of the 13 competitions. Russian swimmer Vladimir Salnikov became the first athlete ever to break 15 minutes for 1500 metres on his way to collecting three gold medals.

British world record holder Sebastian Coe arrived at the Olympics firm favourite to win the 800 metres. His arch-rival, fellow Briton Steve Ovett, declared himself 90 per cent certain to win at his favoured distance, the 1500 metres. Having avoided each other in the heats and semi-finals of the 800 metres, their first meeting came in the final.

A lap into the race, Ovett found himself boxed in and back in sixth place, with Coe trailing the field. Elbows flying and on the verge of disqualification, Ovett pushed his way to second place while Coe wasted time going round the field. Ovett then made his move and with 70 metres to go was clear of the field. Coe pressed on, out-sprinting Belarusian Nikolai Kirov for second place, three metres behind a victorious Ovett. Despite taking the silver medal, Coe considered this the most disappointing day of his athletics career.

The tables would be turned six days later as the two athletes met again in the final of the 1500 metres, where Ovett was by far the favoured athlete having won 42 consecutive races at the distance.

Coe, determined to avoid a repeat of his tactical disaster in the 800 metres, matched Ovett stride for stride. On the final curve Coe unleashed his sprint, passing East German Jürgen Straub. Ovett responded but was no match for Coe's 12.1 second final 100 metres, finishing third behind Straub. Coe had got his revenge and a deserved gold medal.

**BELOW** Sebastian Coe of Great Britain leads team mates Steve Cram and Steve Ovett in the final of the 1500 metres

# Moses

When 20-year-old Edwin Moses arrived in Montreal to run in the 1976 Olympic 400 metres hurdles, few would have known that prior to March 27 of that same year he had only competed at that distance once in his life. A physics and engineering student at Atlanta's Morehouse College, Moses coached himself using local high school facilities as his own college had no track.

With Ugandan reigning world record holder John Akii-Bua forced to stay away as part of the African Nations boycott and Great Britain's Alan Pascoe still suffering the effects of a leg injury, the relatively unknown Moses grabbed his chance of Olympic glory. Using his unique 13-step stride pattern, he demolished the field, winning by an enormous eight metres and setting a new world record time of 47.63 seconds.

Unable to compete at the Moscow Games of 1980, Moses returned to Olympic competition in Los Angeles. Between August 1977 and the start of the 1984 Games he had competed in 102 races, winning every one of them. An unquestionable favourite, Moses lived up to expectations to take his second Olympic gold medal despite being heavily distracted at the start by the clicking of camera shutters.

Moses final Olympic appearance was at the Seoul Games of 1988. In a close competition, he was relegated to a bronze medal having been outrun for gold by compatriot Danny Harris, the Olympic silver medallist in 1984 and the first athlete to break Moses' winning streak a year earlier.

**RIGHT** Ed Moses in action during the Mens 400 metres Hurdles

# Munich 1972

For all their athletic success, the Berlin Olympics of 1936 are forever tainted by the dark shadow of Nazi Germany. It is difficult to look at a photograph of those Games without your attention being drawn to a military uniform or a swastika flag. As the opening of the 1972 Munich Games drew near, the German nation, all too aware of these connotations, set about ensuring these games would be the greatest in history.

On 26 August 1972, the Games of the XX Olympiad were declared open as German athlete Gunther Zahn lit the Olympic flame. With 7,173 athletes from 121 nations attending, a record on both counts, it seemed that the German organisers had achieved their goal. The games continued in peace and harmony for a further nine days until the early hours of September 5.

Between the hours of 4am and 5am, members of the Palestinian terrorist organisation Black September entered an apartment building at 31 Connolly Strasse in the Olympic Village. It was here that members of the Israeli team were sleeping.

As the terrorists stormed the accommodation, wrestling trainer Moshe

Weinberger was gunned down and killed. Weightlifter Yossef Romano was then shot as he tried to raise the alarm. He died later that day from his wounds. Only three Israeli athletes managed to escape; the remaining nine athletes and officials were taken hostage.

The terrorists published their demands –

**ABOVE** Sixteen Year old Ulrike Meyfarth on her way to winning a gold medal in the high jump

# MUNICH 1972

**RIGHT** Valery Borzov winning the Gold Medal in the men's 100 metres

the unconditional release of 234 Palestinians detained in Israel and safe passage for themselves out of Germany. Avery Brundage, chairman of the IOC, announced "the Games must go on" but, with the situation worsening, competition was suspended at 3:51pm.

Negotiations took place all through the day then finally, at 10:10pm, the terrorists and their hostages emerged from the apartments to board a waiting coach, which in turn transported them to three nearby helicopters.

As the helicopters took off, the German authorities entered the building to find the body of Weinberger and three Palestinians suffering from serious stab wounds.

The helicopters flew to meet a waiting Boeing 727 at Fürstenfeldbruck military airbase. Once on the ground, as the terrorists ushered their prisoners towards the waiting airliner, concealed German snipers opened fire. The intention was simple: kill the terrorists and free the hostages.

Despite early reports to the contrary, things went badly wrong. In the gun battle that followed, all nine Israeli athletes, five terrorists and a policeman were killed. Incredibly, considering the location and the security involved, three members of Black September escaped.

The next day a crowd of 80,000 attended a memorial service at the Olympic stadium. Brundage insisted that "peace must prevail over violence", so it was announced the games would continue one day behind schedule.

In spite of the horrific events of September 5 , there were some true athletic highlights at the Munich Games. Within a single week 22-year-old American swimmer Mark Spitz won an incredible seven gold medals, with a world record time in each event. This success took his career Olympic medal tally to 11 medals, nine of them gold.

A 17-year-old Belarusian, Olga Korbut, won the hearts of all who watched her as she recovered from failure to take two gold medals and one silver in the Gymnastics competition. Another young athlete, West German Ulrike Meyfarth, won the women's high jump competition at the age of 16, becoming the youngest winner of an individual athletics event in Olympic history.

But chaos and controversy reigned as the USA and the USSR met in the basketball final. With three seconds remaining, a trailing USA were awarded two free throws. Both were scored and the Americans took the lead 50-49.

With a single second remaining, Soviet coach Vladimir Kondrashkin ran to the referee insisting that he had called a time-out and had not been heard. At the insistence of the FIBA chairman, a time-out was given but as the two seconds had not been put back on the clock the buzzer sounded immediately.

The Americans were jubilant, their fans invading the court. However, the FIBA chairman once again intervened, insisting the missing three seconds be put back on the clock. The time was reset, allowing the Russians to inbound the ball straight to Aleksandr Belov, who scored unopposed. For the first time ever, the American basketball team had been defeated.

**ABOVE** One of the Black September guerrillas who broke into the Munich Olympic Village, killed two members of the Israeli team and took nine others hostage. Eventually all the hostages were killed after a pitched battle at Munich Airport

# Nurmi

Known as the Phantom Finn, Paavo Nurmi was born in Turku in June 1897. An athlete of incredible endurance, he dominated middle and long distance running in the 1920s, always competing with a stopwatch in his hand.

Nurmi's inaugural Olympics were the 1920 Antwerp Games. Competing in his first event, the 5,000 metres, he was out-sprinted in the last 200 metres by Frenchman Joseph Guillemot but managed to collect a silver medal as consolation. Three days later, the tables were turned as Nurmi won gold in the 10,000 metres, with rival Guillemot taking the silver.

Next, competing in the now discontinued cross-country, he won his third and fourth gold medals in the individual and team competitions.

Nurmi achieved an incredible feat at the 1924 Paris Games. Setting off at a blistering pace, he set an Olympic record time in the 1500 metres to take the gold medal then, just one hour later, returned to the track to take victory in the 5,000 metres. Later in the competition, Nurmi won three more gold medals, winning gold in the 3,000 metres team race and both individual and team honours in the cross country.

Nurmi's final Olympic appearance was in Amsterdam at the 1928 Games, where he achieved his ninth gold medal by winning the 10,000 metres and silver medals in the 5,000 metres and the 3,000 metres steeplechase.

Nurmi's record of nine career Olympic gold medals is shared only by three other athletes and bettered by only one.

# Oldest and Youngest

**BELOW** Oscar Swahn, the oldest person ever to win an Olympic medal

Greek Dimitrious Loundrous was only ten years, 218 days when he finished third in the team parallel bars at the 1896 Games, and Italy's Luigina Giavotta won a women's team gymnastics silver medal in 1928 aged just 11 years, 302 days.

There is, though, a mystery surrounding the identity of a young Parisian boy who might be the youngest ever medallist. Drafted in at the last moment, he coxed Dutch rowers Roelof Klein and François Antoine Brandt to victory in the coxed pairs at the 1900 Paris Games and then, after posing for a victory photograph, disappeared back to the streets of Paris. How old was he? No one knows; the best guesses are between seven and 12.

American springboard diver Marjorie Gestring, at 13 years and 268 days, remains the youngest Olympic individual gold medallist. Kusuo Kitamura of Japan holds the record as the youngest male Olympic individual gold medallist; he was just 14 years, 309 days old when he took victory in the 1500 metres at the 1932 Games.

Oscar Swahn of Sweden was the oldest ever Olympic gold medallist, winning the team single-shot running deer shooting in 1912 at 64 years, 257 days. Astoundingly, Swahn returned to the Games in Antwerp to take a silver in the same event, making him, at 72 years, 279 days, the oldest Olympic competitor ever.

The oldest female competitor was Lorna Johnstone who, at the age of 70 years and five days, competed for the Great Britain equestrian dressage team at Munich in 1972.

# Owens

**BELOW** Jesse Owens captures the gold in the long jump event during Olympic Games in Berlin 1936

Jesse Owens is an Olympic legend. Born in Alabama, he first came to athletic prominence at the age of 21 when, at the Michigan Big Ten Championships, he broke five world records and equalled a sixth within the space of 45 minutes.

His most famous achievements occurred at the 1936 Berlin Olympics in the heart of Nazi Germany and in the presence of Adolf Hitler. Owens breezed through the qualifying heats of the 100 metres, equalling the Olympic record in the first round. In the final he fought off a strong challenge from countryman Ralph Metcalfe to take the gold medal in 10.3 seconds.

Qualification for the long jump was not as easy, with Owens fouling his first two attempts. German Luz Long approached him and suggested that if he took off early he could still easily make the distance. Taking the advice of his rival, Owens qualified by just one centimetre.

The two athletes matched each other jump for jump in the final, and it took an enormous leap of 8.06 metres by Owens to secure the gold medal from Long.

Competing in the 200 metres final, Owens controlled the race from start to finish and was barely challenged as he sped his way to a third gold medal of the Games.

A fourth gold medal was easily won in the 4x100 metres relay despite controversy surrounding Owens' and Metcalfe's last-minute selection over Marty Glickman and Sam Stoller, the only two Jewish athletes on the US track team.

Owens' astonishing and symbolic achievement in the heart of Nazi Germany remains one of the most endearing images in Olympic history.

# Paralympics

More than 4,000 athletes, representing around 150 countries, are expected to compete at the 2012 London Paralympic Games, which will run alongside that year's summer Olympics. It's extraordinary to think that this festival of sport for athletes with disabilities stems from an event at which a mere 130 competitors from two countries took part.

Three years after the end of World War II, the eminent neurologist Sir Ludwig 'Poppa' Guttmann organised a sports competition for war veterans under his care at Stoke Mandeville Hospital in Buckinghamshire. Sir Ludwig believed sport was excellent therapy for his victims of spinal cord injury, and his beliefs served to found a worldwide movement.

In 1952, competitors from the Netherlands swelled the number of athletes at the Stoke Mandeville Games to 130, and in 1960 the Games were staged alongside that year's Olympic Games in Rome. Still confined to competitors with spinal injuries, the Rome Paralympics nonetheless attracted 400 athletes from 23 countries.

In Toronto in 1976, athletes with other disabilities – visual impairment and amputees – were accommodated for the first time and by 1988 the idea that the Paralympics should always run alongside the Olympic Games was established. After all, the Greek preposition 'para' means 'beside'. The awe-inspiring spectacle that was the Beijing Paralympic Games in 2008 attracted nearly 4,000 athletes from 146 countries.

Nowadays, Paralympic competition is organised in six categories, into one of which the athletes fall: amputee, cerebral palsy, intellectual disability, visually impaired, wheelchair and Les Autres (The Others). The last category caters for athletes who do not fall into one of the other categories, and covers disabilities including those arising from multiple sclerosis, dwarfism and congenital conditions.

But within those six categories there are, of course, many levels of disability, and it is the job of the International Paralympic Committee, the Games' governing body, to determine what impact an athlete's impairment has on him or her, and decide in which events he or she can compete with peers.

And the range of events is wide. The Summer Paralympic Games consist of 20 sports and roughly 420 events, taking into account all categories and levels of impairment. Wheelchair-bound athletes compete in basketball, fencing, rugby and tennis events; there are indoor football competitions for the visually impaired and those with cerebral palsy; swimming and athletics events take place in five categories; and cycling, equestrian, rowing, sailing and shooting events in four categories each.

Goalball is designed for visually impaired competitors while boccia is another ball game in which wheelchair-bound athletes compete.

In the UK, the Paralympians Tanni Grey-Thompson and Mike Kenny are known for each winning 16 medals, of every hue, but they are far from being the most successful of Paralympics competitors. That honour goes to the American swimmer Trischa Zorn, who collected an extraordinary 55 medals – 41 of them gold – in a career spanning seven Games.

# Paris 1900

Following the undisputed success of the 1896 Athens Games, a large number of people shared the opinion that the Greek capital should play host to the Olympic Games on a permanent basis. But under pressure from president and founder of the modern Olympic movement Baron de Coubertin, the International Olympic Committee agreed that the 1900 Games should be awarded to Paris as part of the World Fair.

Seen as a supporting event and with competition spread from July to October, the Games were referred to as the 'Paris Championships' – many competitors lived and died unaware that they had participated in the Olympics. The Games, though, were not entirely without their highlights.

A 23-year-old American, Alvin Kraenzheim, became the first Olympian to win four gold medals by taking the 60 metres sprint, 100 metres, 200 metres hurdles and the long jump. The last of those events was won controversially as his prime adversary, fellow American Meyer Prinstein, refused to jump in the final as it fell on a Sunday.

Fast times were the order of the day in the swimming events, largely due to the fact that they took place in the River Seine – with the current.

Women competed in the Games for the first time, with British tennis player Charlotte Cooper becoming the inaugural female champion.

**ABOVE** A portrait of British tennis player Charlotte Cooper

# Phelps

We're going to need a bigger record book. The American swimmer Michael Phelps threatens to add to his tally of superlatives every time he dives into a pool. And with the London Olympic Games coming up in 2012, there is every reason to believe the records are going to be rewritten again.

The Baltimore Bullet is already out on his own in the table of male Olympic medal winners. He has won 16 pieces of metalware – a record bettered only by the female Russian-Ukrainian gymnast Larisa Latynina – and included in that number are an astonishing 14 golds. Phelps simply doesn't go in for silver or bronze.

Remember, so far Phelps has only competed in two Olympic gatherings, at Athens in 2004 and Beijing in 2008. To put that gold medal total of 14 in perspective, it's worth recalling that athlete Carl Lewis needed four Olympic tournaments to take his tally up to nine.

But Phelps' records don't stop there. He was, unsurprisingly, the most successful competitor at both the Athens and Beijing Games. He has twice emulated the record of eight medals of any kind won at a single Games, set by Russian gymnast Alexander Dityatin in 1980. He holds the record for the most gold medals won in individual events, with nine. He won more golds (eight) in Beijing than any other athlete has managed at a single edition of the Games. It's not possible to do justice to his achievements in a book of this size.

It has to be said that Phelps has nature on his side. When you look at his physical make-up, it's easier to understand how he

has managed to achieve so much.

His extraordinarily long arms – they span 201cm, while he is 193cm tall – act like highly efficient paddles, aided by his flipper-like size 14 feet. It's thought his relatively short legs lower drag and act like a hydrofoil. He has incredibly flexible ankles, allowing him to whip those huge feet through the water and impart massive thrust. His long, slim torso lowers the water's drag effect, too.

Add to those physical attributes a steely determination to win and intense focus on the job in hand and you have a medal-winning machine.

Fellow swimmer Mark Spitz – himself the winner of nine Olympic medals and therefore no mean judge – has no doubt about Phelps' place in the sporting pantheon. He calls him "the greatest swimmer of all time and the greatest Olympian of all time … maybe the greatest athlete of all time."

No wonder tickets for the swimming events at London 2012 sold out in an instant. Phelps says he might try some new events in London, and it will probably be his last Olympics. Some swimmers will be breathing sighs of relief.

# Pinsent

The date was 21 August 2004, the place the Schinias Olympic Rowing and Canoeing Centre near the ancient Greek town of Marathon. The tension was tangible as the British and Canadian crews vied for the lead over the six minutes it took them to complete the two kilometres of the final of the men's coxless fours at the Athens Olympic Games.

To the millions watching breathlessly on TV the lead seemed to change hands with every stroke as the combatants fought their way to the line, and at the end of a draining race there were a mere eight hundredths of a second between the two crews. Matthew Pinsent, the stroke of the British four, wasn't sure which crew had won, and it took the loud cheers of the British supporters to force home the realisation that he had won his fourth Olympic gold medal.

The tension of the defining moment of the Athens regatta broke and Pinsent, with the knowledge that the surge of his crew's final stroke had made the difference between gold and silver, wept. He had become one of only five athletes to win Olympic gold at four consecutive tournaments. He was shortly to retire, and to become Sir Matthew Pinsent, knight bachelor.

In winning three of those four golds, he had been associated with fellow rowing knight Steve Redgrave. The first came in 1992, when the pair competed in the coxless pairs in Barcelona and saw off the challenge of the German and Slovenian crews, winning by a good five seconds. Pinsent was just 21 years old.

There was a repeat performance in 1996 at Lake Lanier, Georgia, when Pinsent and Redgrave beat Australia and France into silver and bronze medal positions respectively.

At the Sydney Games of 2000, the pair, by

**RIGHT** Gold medal winner Matthew Pinsent

now both rowing superstars in the eyes of the British public, moved up to the coxless fours to partner James Cracknell and Tim Foster. The final was a desperately close-run thing, with the Britons claiming victory over the Italian crew by just four tenths of a second and Pinsent getting his hands on his third gold. That race was later voted Britain's greatest sporting moment.

And so to Athens, where he teamed up with Cracknell, Steve Williams and Ed Coode. The Olympics followed a difficult year of highs and lows, but what a finish.

Pinsent is a giant of a man at 6ft 8in, and his enormous lung capacity of 8.5 litres saw him through a rowing career that started at Eton, continued through three Boat Races while at Oxford and saw him claim ten gold medals in the world championships – seven of them in partnership with Redgrave. None of them meant as much as that final Olympic gold in Athens.

**LEFT** Matthew Pinsent and the rest of his team celbrating their gold medal win.

# Quick off the Blocks

**BELOW** Donovan Baily, winning the men's 100m in a new world record of 9.84 seconds at the Olympic Stadium at the 1996 Centennial Olympic Games in Atlanta, Georgia

Seen as the premier event of the Olympic Games, the 100 metres never fails to capture the imagination. In this event of outright power, athletes do not even take time to breathe from the moment the gun fires until they have crossed the finish line.

The first Olympic 100 metres champion was American Thomas Burke. Victorious with a 12.0 seconds run, he had wowed a curious Greek public with his pioneering crouched starting position.

Great Britain won its first Olympic 100 metres at the 1924 Paris Games. As film fans saw in Chariots of Fire, Harold Abrahams, having hired the services of legendary coach Harold Mussabini, stormed to victory, equalling the Olympic record of 10.6 seconds.

The eventful 1936 Olympics saw the powerful Nazi propaganda machine confounded by the 100 metres triumph of African-American Jesse Owens, to the delight of the Berlin crowd.

Assisted by the rarefied atmosphere of the Mexico City Stadium, American James Hines sped to victory in a word record time of 9.95 seconds at the 1968 Games. His time would not be bettered in Olympic competition until Carl Lewis recorded 9.90 seconds at the 1988 Seoul Games following Canadian Ben Johnson's disqualification drug use.

Britain's Linford Christie, at 32 years old, became the oldest ever winner of the 100 metres at the 1992 Barcelona Olympics recording 9.96 seconds. Usain Bolt's incredible 9.69 seconds in Beijing in 2008 – achieved with no following wind, while one of Bolt's shoelaces was undone and with the Jamaican slowing to celebrate in the final few metres – remains the Olympic record.

# Racquet Sports

Three forms of racquet sport are contested at the Olympic Games – tennis, table tennis and badminton.

Tennis first featured in the Olympics at the Athens Games of 1896, with a women's competition being added in 1900. Charlotte Cooper of Great Britain, a five times Wimbledon champion, was not only the first winner of the women's tennis tournament but also the first female champion of the modern Olympics.

Despite its popularity, tennis was dropped from the Olympic programme following the Paris Games of 1924 due to issues of professionalism. It would be another 60 years before tennis would again feature at the Olympics, first as a demonstration sport in 1984 and then as a full medal sport in 1988, at which point professionals were permitted to take part.

Germany's Steffi Graff, winner of the 1984 demonstration tournament despite being its youngest competitor, arrived at the 1988 Olympic Games ranked number one in the world. That year she had won the Australian

**BELOW** The finals of the men's singles badminton finals during the 2004 Olympics

Open, French Open, Wimbledon and, just a week prior to the Games, the US Open. To this she added an Olympic gold medal, beating Argentinean Gabriella Sabatini in straight sets.

Considering the Asian nations' passion for the game of table tennis, it seems appropriate that its inclusion in the Olympics started at the 1988 Seoul Games. To the delight of a more than enthusiastic home crowd, the first men's singles final was an all-Korean affair between Yoo Nam-Kyu and Kim Ki-Taik.

Asian dominance of the sport was further demonstrated in the women's singles competition at the 1996 Atlanta Games, at which 11 of the 63 competitors were of Chinese birth.

Although it remains a topic of debate, it is said that the sport of badminton was invented in the mid-1800s at Badminton House in Gloucestershire, although the location is now more readily associated with equestrianism.

Badminton made an appearance as a demonstration sport at the 1972 Munich Games before gaining acceptance as a full Olympic sport for male and female competitors at Barcelona in 1992.

Matches are played as the best of three sets, a set being won by the first player to reach 15 points in men's and doubles competition or 11 points in the women's competition.

# Redgrave

When a 22-year-old Steve Redgrave rowed to an Olympic gold medal as a member of the coxed fours at the 1984 Los Angeles Games, few people can have realised that 20 years later he would be considered Britain's greatest ever Olympian.

Born in Buckinghamshire, Redgrave was always seen as being single-minded in his quest for success. His ability and willingness to work through pain and beyond his own physical threshold set him apart from other athletes, who could only hope to emulate his drive and determination.

Paired with Andrew Holmes, Redgrave achieved his second Olympic gold medal in the coxless pairs at the 1988 Seoul Games. Less than 24 hours later, he and Holmes rowed to a bronze medal in the coxed pairs.

Redgrave returned from the 1992 Barcelona Games with a third gold medal, having partnered Matthew Pinsent to victory in the coxless pairs. In doing so he had become only the third British athlete to earn gold medals in three consecutive

Olympics, and the partnership he forged with Pinsent was to reap staggering levels of success.

Teaming up again with Pinsent, he returned to Olympic competition in Atlanta to collect his fourth gold medal in the pair's 100th race as a partnership, following which he famously

**ABOVE** Steve Redgrave of Great Britain holds his Five Olympic Gold Medals

declared to the TV cameras: "Anyone who sees me go anywhere near a boat again, ever, you've got my permission to shoot me."

Redgrave fought serious illnesses for lengthy periods of his career, shrugging them off to continue training and competing. First, in 1992, he discovered he had ulcerative colitis then, in 1997, he was diagnosed as a Type 1 diabetic. It is typical of his determination that, despite these setbacks, on 23 September 2000 he, Pinsent, James Cracknell and Tim Foster powered their way to victory over a closing Italian team in the final of the Olympic coxless fours. In doing so, Redgrave became only the fourth athlete in history to win gold medals at five different Games.

Journalist Simon Barnes was one of those who were marvelling at Redgrave's seemingly limitless reserves of strength, skill and grit, and he described that Sydney performance as "the greatest piece of sport I have ever seen. I am not challenging for originality here: it was the greatest piece of sport anybody has ever seen."

Sir Steve Redgrave – he was knighted in 2001, to the surprise of absolutely nobody – has not finished with the Olympic Games, despite his retirement from competitive rowing in 2000. With the Games coming to London in 2012, he has been appointed Sports Legacy Champion, a role that sees him helping with the drive to get more people playing sport. Sadly, we can say for certain that none of those people, inspired though they might be by the legend that is Steve Redgrave, will ever approach his greatness.

# Relatively speaking

There is a long history of both rivalry and co-operation among relatives at the Olympics. At the inaugural Athens Games in 1896, American brothers John and Sumner Paine finished first and second in the military revolver shooting.

Four years later in Paris, the Doherty brothers, representing Great Britain, were due to meet in the semi-finals of the men's singles tennis competition. Reginald stepped aside, forfeiting the match and allowing his brother Laurie to rest for the final, which he subsequently won. Reginald then defeated Arthur Norris in the minor final to take the bronze medal. Both players then went forward to win the doubles competition.

During the Antwerp Games of 1920, Italian fencer Neo Nadi won an astounding five gold medals, while his younger brother Aldo collected three gold medals and one silver.

American rower Bill Havens forfeited his seat in the coxed eights at the 1924 Games to stay at home with his pregnant wife. In 1952, Frank Havens, the son born during those Olympics, won a gold medal in the 10,000 metres Canadian singles canoeing, while at the 1948 Games the star-class yachting was won by American father and son Hillary and Paul Smart.

A true family effort was displayed in the cycling team time trial at the 1968 Games, during which Swedish brothers Erik, Gösta, Sture and Tomas Pettersson secured silver medals.

**BELOW** The Italian Fencing team including Aldo Nadi (centre left) and Nedo Nadi (centre right) posing during the 1920 Olympic Games in Antwerp, Belgium

# Rome 1960

The 1960 Rome Games were to be a proud moment for the Italian capital, 54 years after it had been readying itself for the Olympics.

The Vesuvius eruption of 1906 had meant that the planned Rome Games of 1908 had been cancelled and reassigned to London. With typical Italian style, and the obligatory blessing from Pope John XXIII, the Romans set about presenting an Olympic showcase of epic proportions.

Wrestlers competed in the Basilica de Maxentius, where bouts had been fought two thousand years before, while the gymnasts performed in the ancient Caracalla Baths.

The fourth-century Arch of Constantine provided the stunning backdrop for the finish of the marathon – the first to be run at night. With the way lit by torches held by Italian soldiers, it was here that barefoot Ethiopian Abebe Bikila took Olympic marathon victory and in doing so became the first black African Olympic gold medallist.

A resurgent German team surprised many by beating the United States in the rowing coxed eights and on the track in the 4x100m relay. America had won every Olympic final in both events since 1920.

To cap these fine performances, another German, Armin Hary, beat American David Sime to win the blue riband 100 metre sprint.

# Rowing

Rowing has been an Olympic sport since the Paris Games of 1900, and women's events were introduced to the programme at the Montreal Games of 1976.

The competition distance changed several times over the years, until 2,000 metres was agreed for both men's and women's events at the 1992 Barcelona Games. Two types of rowing – sculls and sweeps – are contested in Olympic competition.

Sculls are contested individually, as pairs and as fours by both men and women (albeit in separate competitions), with each sculler pulling a pair of 2.98 metre sculling blades.

Sweeps are raced in pairs and eights by women and men and as fours by men only. In all variations, the rowers pull a 3.82 metre-long single oar with its blade painted in the national colours of the team.

The men's eight also requires the use of a

**BELOW** James Cracknell, Steve Redgrave, Tim Foster and Matthew Pinsent of Great Britain cross the line to win Gold in the Men's Coxless Four Rowing Final ahead of Italy (Silver) and Australia (Bronze)

coxswain, whose job it is to steer the boat. There is a minimum weight for coxswains of 55kg. If a coxswain is found to be underweight, ballast may be added to the boat to remove any advantage in the water.

In 1996, a lightweight class was added to the programme with a lightweight coxless four for men and lightweight double-sculls competitions for men and women. To qualify for the lightweight class, male rowers must weigh no more than 72.5kg and

female competitors no more than 59kg; but in addition the average weight of a crew may not exceed 70kg for men's crews and 57kg for women's.

The rowing competitions consist of a qualifying round, from which the fastest 12 boats progress to the semi-finals. The three fastest semi-finalists in each round move forward to take part in the final, with the remaining six teams contesting a 'petit final' to establish positions down to 12th place.

# Sailing

**LEFT** John Lovell and Charlie Ogeltree of USA in action sail their way to silver in the open multihull tornado finals race 4 during the Athens 2004 Summer Olympic Games

Sailing is the only Olympic sport in which men and women are permitted to compete against each other. Competitors sail in a series of races with points being awarded depending on their placing. The first place crew scores one point, the second placed two points and so on. The crew with the lowest cumulative score wins the competition.

The classes of craft used in Olympic sailing are divided into four groups – windsurfer, dinghy, keel boat and catamaran.

Windsurfing was first introduced into the Games in 1984. Currently this class utilises the Mistral One type of board, a 4.24 metre-long board topped with a 7.4 square metre sail.

The dinghy category utilises the single sail (una) rigged Finn, Europe and Laser classes and the two sail (sloop) rigged 49er and 470 classes. Dinghies are steered by a rudder with the crew using body weight to counterbalance the craft.

The Solling and Star classes are categorised as keel boats, named after the ballasted fin fixed to the hull. The Solling, requiring a crew of three, is the largest craft used in Olympic sailing at 8.2 metres in length.

The Tornado is the only catamaran used in Olympic competition. These are twin-hulled craft with a sloop rig and a fixed mainsail and are the fastest of the sailing classes with the exception of the windsurfers.

# Seoul 1988

**RIGHT** An offical poster from the 1988 Seoul Olympic Games

It has been said that politics have a detrimental effect on the Olympics. In the case of the 1988 Seoul Games, however, there was a clear demonstration of how the Olympics can have a positive effect on politics. In order to satisfy international opinion and with the eyes of the world watching, the ruling South Korean dictatorship abdicated in favour of democratic elections.

Great drama surrounded the opening ceremony. The Olympic torch entered the stadium in the hand of 76-year-old Sohn Kee-chung, winner of the marathon at the 1936 Berlin Games where, due to the military occupation of Korea, he had been forced to run under the Japanese name of Son Kitei. Far from showing his advancing years, Sohn sprinted into the stadium filled with pride.

Making its Olympic appearance for the first time, the table tennis competition was dominated by the host nation and the Chinese. On the grass courts, tennis made a return to the games after a 64-year absence, bringing with it some of the biggest names in the sport. Singles gold medals were awarded to Slovakian Miloslav Mecír in the men's tournament and West Germany's Steffi Graf in the women's.

East German Kristin Otto caused a sensation in the pool, winning six gold medals with victories in the 50m and 100m freestyle, 100m backstroke, 100m butterfly, 4x100 freestyle and 4x100 medley.

As Otto had dominated the women's swimming events, so six-foot six-inch American Matt Biondi stood out in the men's competition. In an outstanding series of performances, Biondi won seven medals, five of them gold, taking the top spot on the rostrum for the 50m and 100m freestyle, 4x100m and 4x200m relays and the 4x100m medley.

Further excitement poolside was generated by diver Greg Louganis of the United States, who became the first man in Olympic history to win both the springboard and platform diving competitions – despite hitting his head against the board during the preliminary rounds.

By far the biggest story of the 1988 Games was that of Canadian sprinter Ben Johnson who, after setting a new world record in the final of the 100 metres sprint, tested positive for the banned steroid stanozolol. Although there had been positive tests in previous Olympic Games, this was the first time such a major name had been caught. Johnson returned to Canada in disgrace, with Carl Lewis of the United States being awarded the gold medal.

In the women's track competition, American Florence Griffith-Joyner, known to the world as Flo-Jo, took victory first in the 100m, then the 200m, recording world record times in the semi-final and final. She achieved a third gold medal in the 4x100m relay.

# Stockholm 1912

**BELOW** A general view of the stadium used for the 1912 Stockholm Olympics

Many new innovations were brought to the fore at the Stockholm Games of 1912. Electronic timing devices were used, albeit unofficially, for the track events and a public address system kept spectators and competitors informed of events.

Women's swimming was introduced for the first time, with Australian Sarah 'Fanny' Durack claiming victory in the 100m freestyle despite having been required to cover her own expenses to attend.

Success in the women's 4x100m freestyle relay went to the British team of Isabella Moore, Jennie Fletcher, Annie Speirs and Irene Steer.

Two battles of epic proportions were fought in the Greco-Roman wrestling tournament. Finland's Ivar Böling and Swede Anders Ahlgren grappled for an incredible nine hours in the light-heavyweight final before judges declared a draw. Olympic rules stated that it was necessary for a winner to defeat his adversary, so it was decided that both men should be awarded silver medals.

A semi-final bout in the middleweight category saw Estonian Martin Klein and Finn Alfred Asikainen wrestle for 11 hours before Klein eventually pinned his opponent and claimed the win. Unfortunately, the effort had exhausted him so much that he was unable to take part in the final, and victory went to Swedish competitor Claes Johanson by default.

# Sydney 2000

Immaculately conceived and executed, the Sydney 2000 Olympics came as a welcome tonic after the poorly organised and overtly commercialised Atlanta Games four years previously. The Australian population understood the importance of the millennium Games in the eyes of the world, and in return presented an Olympic experience bigger, brighter and better than any that had gone before.

A hundred and ninety nine nations, the greatest number ever, were represented by a record 10,651 athletes, who competed in 300 events across 29 sports; 47,000 volunteers kept the Games ticking like clockwork, while 16,000 members of the media kept global audiences informed.

In an impressive opening ceremony, 120 Australian stock-horses performed to a capacity crowd in the 110,000-seat, purpose-built Olympic stadium before Kathy Freeman, an Australian athlete of Aboriginal descent, lit the Olympic flame. Freeman filled the spotlight again just ten days later during what turned out to be one of the greatest nights in athletic history.

Freeman won the women's 400 metres final by four metres from Jamaican Lorraine Graham in front of a crowd of 112,524. In the next race, American Michael Johnson took victory in the 400 metres to become the Games' first repeat winner at the distance.

Britain's Jonathan Edwards won the triple jump after a disappointing performance in Atlanta and Maria Mutola of Mozambique, competing in her fourth Games, snatched victory in the women's 800m to win her first Olympic gold medal.

But the highlight of the evening was to be the final of the men's 10,000m. Ethiopian world record holder Haile Gebrselassie had not lost at the distance in seven years but had missed three months of preparation due to injury. An electrifying race ensued.

With 250 metres to go, Kenyan Paul Tergat raced to the front with Gebrselassie in pursuit until, with only 50 metres remaining, he pulled alongside Tergat. The Kenyan fought back, Gebrselassie holding level until his final strides when the Ethiopian dipped forward to take the gold medal by just nine-hundredths of a second.

Competing at his first Olympic Games, Australia's Ian Thorpe broke two world

**ABOVE** Jonathan Edwards celebrates Gold in the Triple Jump final

**RIGHT** Horseriders carry Olympic flags during the opening ceremony of the Sydney 2000 Olympic Games

**BELOW** Cathy Freeman cruises to victory to take the gold medal in a special body suit in the Women's 400m final

records in the space of one hour. The first saw him win the 400 metres by almost three seconds from Italian Massimiliano Rosolino; the second, as part of the Australian 4x100 metres relay team, put an end to the United States' unbeaten record in the event.

More was expected of 'the Thorpedo' in the 200 metres freestyle, but the gold medal was won by 22-year-old Dutchman Pieter Van den Hoogenband, who in doing so set a world record for himself. Just two days later, Van den Hoogenband completed a medal double by defeating Russian great Aleksandr Popov in the 100 metres freestyle.

For Great Britain, the outstanding moment of the games came on September 23. With the entire nation watching on TV, the team of James Cracknell, Tim Foster, Matthew Pinsent and Steve Redgrave rowed their way to victory in the coxless fours. With this victory, 38-year-old Redgrave became only the fourth athlete ever to earn gold medals at five different Olympic Games.

Stevenson's place was always among the amateurs. It was also in the hearts of boxing

fans, who saw him take gold medals, at heavyweight, at three consecutive Olympics. It could perhaps have been four if Cuba had not followed the Soviet Union's lead and boycotted the 1984 Games in Los Angeles.

By the end of his career, Stevenson had fought 302 times and lost only 22 times, but none were as highly valued as the Olympic contests.

First, at Munich in 1972, he progressed steadily to the final, dealing with the threat of American Duane Bobick – later to have a distinguished professional career – along the way. Stevenson was gifted the gold medal when the injured Romanian Ion Alexe was unable to appear.

By the time he won his second Olympic gold at Montreal in 1976, with a technical knockout over Mircea Şimon, he was a national hero in Cuba. His third gold came in 1980 in Moscow, where he defeated the home favourite Piotr Zaev on points.

Not many fighters got the better of Teofilo Stevenson, and not a single one did it inside an Olympic boxing ring.

# Team Sports

If you discount water polo, which is normally grouped among the aquatic sports, five team sports are to be contested at the 2012 Olympic Games in London: basketball, volleyball, football, handball and hockey.

And that means that baseball and softball, last seen at Beijing in 2008, will no longer be part of the Olympic programme. At a meeting of the IOC in 2005, the two sports were voted out of the 2012 Games, becoming the first sports to be thus eliminated since polo was excluded from the 1936 Olympics.

If there are many baseball fans who also relish rugby, they will gain some consolation from 2016, when the sevens version of the game will get an airing in Rio de Janeiro. Rugby, in fact, already has some Olympic history, having been played at the first four versions of the modern Games.

Basketball made its first Olympic appearance at the 1936 Berlin Games in a tournament won, not surprisingly, by the United States of America. They continued to dominate the competition until the 1972 Munich Olympics, at which a determined Soviet team inflicted defeat after controversially scoring in the final seconds.

**BELOW** Grant Schubert of Australia scores on a high shot over the blocker of goaltender Bernardino Herrera of Spain in the men's field hockey semi-final during the Athens 2004 Olympic Games

**MIDDLE** Action in the Women's beach volleyball competition during the 2004 Olympics in Athens

American dominance returned to the competition in 1992 following a decision to allow professional players to participate, allowing the famed Dream Team to be formed and win gold without calling a single time-out. Argentina interrupted America's series of gold medals in 2004, but normal service was resumed in Beijing.

Women's basketball was introduced to the Games in 1976, and gold medal honours have been shared by Soviet and United States teams, with the US proving the better team since the 1996 Atlanta Games. Home team China had to be content with fourth place in 2008, with the US defeating Australia 92-65 in the final.

Olympic basketball is played over four ten-minute periods, with an additional five-minute overtime period being allocated should the game be tied. Both the men's and the women's tournaments are contested by 12 teams who are, with the exception of the host nation and the reigning world champions, required to qualify through a championship the year preceding the Games.

Football has enjoyed a long existence in Olympic history. First appearing at the 1900 Paris Games, it has featured at every Olympiad since with the exception of those held in Los Angeles in 1932.

In 1996, a women's tournament was added to the programme, which was contested by 12 teams when the Games reached Beijing in 2008. The same format will be in force in 2012.

Since 1992, professional players have been eligible to play in Olympic competition provided they are under 23 years old. A team may now also add to its squad a maximum of three professional players over this age restriction.

Olympic gold went to the men of France for the first time in 2008, while Norway claimed the honours in the women's tournament.

Hockey first became an Olympic sport at the 1908 London Games. India dominated the tournament for many years, winning 30 consecutive games to claim six gold medals between 1928 and 1956. Women's hockey was introduced to the Games in 1980.

Both the men's and the women's competitions start with a preliminary round, with the teams split into two pools. The top two teams from each pool progress to the semi-finals while the remaining teams contest classification matches to establish the lesser placings. The winning semi-final teams advance to meet in the final to decide the gold and silver medals, while the semi-final losers play for the bronze.

Last time out, in Beijing, the men's gold medals were taken by Germany for the first time since 1992, while the Netherlands proved the strongest team among the women.

Volleyball has been an Olympic sport since the introduction of men's and women's tournaments at the 1964 Tokyo Games.

Argentina won the men's tournament for the second Games running in 2008, while the women's gold medals were picked up by the strong United States team.

Handball made its Olympic debut at the 1936 Berlin Games, although it did not make a second appearance until the 1972 Munich Games with the women's tournament being introduced in 1976. Handball is a fast-moving game between two teams of seven players contested over two 30-minute halves. Much like basketball, players move the ball by passing and dribbling but the object of the game is to score goals in a defended net rather than a suspended basket.

RIGHT Argentina celebrate after beating Paraguay 1-0 to claim the men's football gold medal in Athens 2004

BELOW Isabel Ortuna of Spain knocks over the Ukrainian defence in the women's handball quarter-final during the Athens 2004 Olympic Games

Twelve teams take part in each tournament, with matches being played as the best of five sets. The first four sets of competition are played to 25 points, with the final set being played to just 15 points, although there must be a clear two-point advantage.

In Beijing, the US team won gold and the Brazilians silver in the men's event, with the result being reversed in the women's tournament.

Although volleyball has always generated a strong following at the Olympics, the introduction of beach volleyball at the 1996 Atlanta Games opened the sport to a whole new audience. Played in pairs rather than teams of 12, beach volleyball players must have excellent co-ordination and stamina to cope with the difficult sandy playing surface. As in 'normal' volleyball, American and Brazilian pairs have proved strong in this event.

# Thompson

Daley Thompson remains one of the best-loved characters in British Olympic history. His trademark moustache, beaming smile and pithy one-liners endeared him to the public and fellow athletes alike.

At 18 years old, Frances Morgan Thompson arrived at the 1976 Montreal Olympics the youngest decathlon competitor, and he finished 18th overall.

Four years later, in Moscow, Thompson had raised his game. The West German boycott of the Olympics had removed the threat of Guido Kratschmer, his greatest rival. With little opposition he set out at a blistering pace, but heavy rain on the second day thwarted any hopes of a world record. Regardless, Thompson demolished the field, finishing 164 points clear.

By the Los Angeles Games of 1984, Thompson had a new West German rival in the form of world record holder Jürgen Hingsen. The two were neck and neck when the crucial moment came in the discus. Thompson made two poor throws whereas Hingsen threw a huge 50.82 metres. Under pressure, Thompson replied with a 46.56 metre throw – enough to secure 100 points and maintain his lead.

Competing in the pole vault, Hingsen complained of feeling ill and underperformed. For Thompson victory was a formality. Cruising home in the 1500m, he then took a victory lap wearing a T-shirt with the message "Thanks America for a good Games and a great time", while on the back it read "But what about the TV coverage?" – a reference to US television only covering the performances of American athletes.

**ABOVE** Daley Thompson clears the bar in the Pole Vault section during the Decathlon event at the 1984 Olympic Games

# Tokyo 1964

TOKYO 1964

**RIGHT** Antonius Geesink of Holland raises his arms in victory after beating Japan's Akio Kaminaga in the final of the Judo non-category class at the 1964 Tokyo Olympics

Nineteen-year-old Japanese athlete Yoshinori Sakai was chosen to light the Olympic flame at the opening of the 1964 Tokyo Games. He had been born in Hiroshima on 6 August 1945, the day the first atomic bomb had been unleashed.

Judo found itself included in the programme for the first time but, to the surprise and embarrassment of the host nation, the gold medal went to Antonius Geesink, a 267-pound, six foot six inch judo instructor from Utrecht, Holland.

Ethiopia's Abebe Bikila retained his marathon title, setting a new world record time in the process and competing less than six weeks after an appendix operation.

Another athlete performing under duress was discus thrower Al Oerter of the United States who, suffering from torn rib cartilage and a cervical disc injury, was forced to wear a neck harness. Despite his discomfort, Oerter threw 61 metres to take the gold medal and an Olympic record.

Ukrainian gymnast Larysa Latynina won six medals, two of each colour, to take her Olympic career total to a stunning 18 medals.

A somewhat unusual record was achieved in the semi-final of the cycling match sprint as Frenchman Pierre Trentin and Giovanni Pettenella of Italy balanced upright for 21 minutes 57 seconds without moving.

# Track and Field

Track and field, otherwise known as athletics, is rightfully considered the backbone of the Olympics featuring, as it does, many of the Blue Riband events of the Games. Just 12 track and field events were contested at the 1896 Athens Olympics but, by the time the Games returned to the Greek capital in 2004, this number had increased almost fourfold to 46 events.

Olympic track and field events can be broken down into six categories: sprints, middle distance, long distance, jumping, throwing and multi-discipline.

The first category incorporates the 100, 200 and 400 metres sprints and the 110 and 400 metres hurdles. The 100 metres is regarded as the most prestigious of Olympic athletic events, and the winner is usually considered the world's fastest man or woman. The profile of the 200 metres has increased considerably over recent years, in part due to the phenomenal record-breaking performances of Michael Johnson in 1996 and Usain Bolt in 2008.

The 400 metres has always been considered a difficult race as it requires immense tolerance to the build-up of lactic acid – the substance that causes that heavy-legged feeling during exercise. Many sprinters have combined the 100 and 200 metres or the 200 and 400 metres, but very few are capable of contesting all three successfully.

Middle distance runners are not only required to be able to cover the ground at

**ABOVE** Action in the final of the women's javelin event at the Athens 2004 Olympics

high speed; they must also be thinkers and tacticians. While sprint races are run close to flat out for their entire distance, these events can be played out at almost any pace from the gun.

Women's events above 400 metres were suspended from 1928 until the Games of 1960 because officials considered the exhaustion it caused the athletes to be unhealthy and dangerous. It is interesting to note that the current best women's 800 metres time would have been fast enough to have give the bronze medal winner in the men's event a run for his money at those 1928 Olympics.

Although they were dominated over many decades by athletes from Finland, Czechoslovakia and the Soviet Union, the long distance events have for some years been the showcase for the top athletes of the African nations.

To run competitively at distances of 5,000 metres and over, the athletes must possess an exceptional level of anaerobic conditioning and complete, uninterrupted mental determination to cope with the ever-changing tactics and long periods of time spent pounding the track. In the words of the great Czech athlete Emile Zátopek, "If you want to win something, run the 100 metres. If you want to experience something, run the marathon."

A curious event exists in the form of the 20,000 and 50,000 metres walks. Competitors are required to keep at least one foot in contact with the ground at all times while ensuring that their leading leg remains straight at the point of first contact.

The jumping category incorporates the high, long and triple jumps in addition to the pole vault. Competitors in the high jump are allowed to choose the height at which their first attempt is made and are permitted three attempts to clear the bar. If an athlete fails to clear the bar they may move on to the next height, but three consecutive failures results in elimination.

Athletes in the long and triple jumps are given three attempts to qualify for a final field of 12 competitors. Should the athlete launch his or her jump after the take-off board, land outside the sand pit or perform any sort of somersault, a no-jump is recorded. A triple jumper must first land on his take-off foot then on his opposite foot before completing the exercise with a jump landing two footed in the pit.

The throwing events consist of the shot, discus, hammer and javelin. The shot is an iron ball, 7.26kg in weight for men and 4kg for women, that is thrown from within a 2.1 metre circle. Each competitor is given three throws to qualify for the final, in which the top eight athletes are given three more attempts.

The discus is the only track and field event whose world record has not been beaten in Olympic competition. The discus is 2kg in weight for men, half that for women, and is thrown from within a 2.5 metre circle.

The hammer is a 7.26kg ball attached to a handle by a 120cm steel wire. Throwers make three to four full rotations in the 2.1 metre hammer circle before launching the ball down the course with an initial velocity in excess of 100 km/h. With all of these events competitors must stay within the circle when executing their throw, exiting to the rear.

Failure to do so results in the attempt being marked as a no-throw.

An Olympic javelin, its shaft constructed of wood or metal, is 2.7 metres in length with a minimum weight of 800g. Throws are made from above the shoulder after a run up of up to 36 metres. For a throw to be declared valid, its tip must break the surface of the ground on impact. In 1986, the world record distance for

**ABOVE** Mary Rand of Great Britain in action during the long jump event at the Olympic Games in Tokyo. She finished with a world record jump of 6.76metres to win the Gold Medal

**ABOVE** Olga Kuzenkova of Russia competes in the women's hammer throw final during the Athens 2004 Olympic Games

the javelin throw was reset after changes were implemented in the design of the javelin itself following a series of dangerously long throws.

There are two multi-sport events contested in Olympic competition. The men's decathlon consists of the 100 metres sprint, long jump, shot put, high jump, 400 metres, 100 metres hurdles, discus, pole vault, javelin and 1500 metres, while the women's heptathlon consists of a 100 metres hurdles, high jump, shot put, 200 metres, long jump, javelin and 800 metres.

The rules used in each event are the same as those for the individual competitions, with the exception that competitors are allowed two false starts instead of one. Points are awarded for each event based on a series of tables approved by the International Amateur Athletics Federation.

# Triathlon

Triathlon made its Olympic debut on the first day of competition at the 2000 Sydney Games in front of a crowd of 200,000 spectators. The sport was invented in 1974 by members of the San Diego Track Club as an alternative to the monotony of track training. Their first event comprised a ten kilometre run, an eight kilometre cycle and a 500m swim.

The distances involved in the Olympic triathlon are somewhat greater. A 1,500 metre open water swim is followed by a 40 kilometres cycle and then a 10,000 metres run, with men and women both competing over the same distances. With the clock running from start to finish, time can often be made up by speedy changes between each element, known as transitions.

Triathletes must wear a coloured cap for identification in the swimming phase, with the use of a wetsuit being dependent on water temperature. If the water is below 14°C a wetsuit is mandatory; between 14°C and 20°C it is optional; and over 20°C it is outlawed. During the cycling element, the use of an approved helmet is compulsory.

Qualification for the Olympic triathlon is based on the athlete's world ranking but is limited to a maximum of three competitors per nation for each of the men's and women's competitions.

**BELOW** The triathlon pack competing in the 40 kilometre distance cycling phase in the Athens 2004 Olympics

# Up and Over

U

**BELOW** Dick Fosbury of the USA clears the bar in the high jump competiton with his dramatic new jumping style

Until 1968, the technique of the high jump had been evolving for many years. The early 20th century had seen extensive use of the western roll developed by American George Horine, in which the jumper approached at an angle, taking off on his inner leg to roll sideways over the bar. This method remained popular up until the Berlin Olympics of 1936.

From the 1948 Games, competition had been dominated by American and Russian high jumpers with the evolution of the straddle jump, in which the athlete rotated his torso around the bar as he rolled over it. The success of Ukrainian world record holder Valery Brumel in this technique saw American coaches travelling to Russia to learn from his coaches.

Then, in 1968, a young American jumper, Dick Fosbury, made his Olympic debut. Practically unknown just a year before, he set the games alight with his revolutionary 'Fosbury Flop'. Approaching the bar at high speed, Fosbury took off on his inside leg, just like everybody else, but then rotated himself on to his back, crossing the bar head first.

Spectators, judges and coaches were amazed as this new star cleared every height through to 2.24 metres to take the Olympic gold medal.

Fosbury never repeated his gold medal glory, but his name will live for ever in Olympic memory; the Fosbury Flop is now considered the standard technique.

# Virén

Lasse Virén was a Flying Finn in the tradition of Olympic greats Hannes Kolehmainen and Paavo Nurmi. A police officer by profession, Virén trained for countless hours in the forests that surrounded his home town of Myrskylä, Finland.

His Olympic debut came in the 10,000 metres at the 1972 Munich Games. Briton David Bedford set off at a blistering world record pace. His strategy had been to blow apart the opposition, but with 4,600 metres covered there were still eight runners with him including Virén.

Disaster struck as the Finn stumbled and fell to the ground, taking Mohamed Gammoudi of Tunisia with him. Quick to his feet, Virén was up to second place within 230 metres. The lead changed several times until, with 600 metres to go, Virén attacked. Nobody had the strength to go with him as he sprinted home to a gold medal and a new world record.

Virén complemented his 10,000 metres victory with a gold medal and Olympic record in the 5,000 metres just days later, to become only the fourth runner to achieve a 5,000/10,000 metres double.

A third gold medal was achieved four years later in the 10,000 metres at the Montreal Games. Portuguese athlete Carlos Lopes took on the field, pulling away from all but Virén, who unleashed his kick with 450 metres remaining to win the gold by 30 metres. Four days later, Virén claimed his fourth Olympic gold, taking victory in the 5,000 metres and becoming the first repeat winner of the event.

**ABOVE** Lasse Virén wins the 5,000-meter run during the Olympic Games held in Montreal

# Weightlifting

Weightlifting was included in the programme of the first Olympic Games in 1896 but was categorised as part of the athletics schedule. It was only in 1920 that it was classified as a sport in its own right.

There have been many variations of the lifts required in Olympic competition. Early Olympics included one-handed lifts and a dumb-bell event. Women's weightlifting was introduced at the 2000 Games.

The current weightlifting programme requires the completion of two lifts: the snatch and the clean-and-jerk. In both phases the competitor chooses at which weight to commence lifting and the subsequent level of increase as the rounds progress, and he or she has three attempts at each lift.

The competitor who lifts the highest combined weight for snatch and clean-and-jerk wins the competition. In the event of a tie, the competitor with the lowest bodyweight wins.

To complete a snatch, the competitor must lift the weight using a wide armed position in one movement from the floor to above his or her head, and hold it still until a signal is given by the referee.

The clean-and-jerk is a two stage lift in which the bar is held with arms at shoulder width. The bar is first drawn to the chest and then lifted to the full stretch of the arms over the competitor's head.

# Wiggins

Cycling legend Lance Armstrong is in no doubt about Bradley Wiggins' credentials and he doesn't mince his words in announcing them. He describes the man who has won six Olympic medals at three different Games as "the best ****ing pursuiter of all time".

Few people would argue with Armstrong's assessment. Wiggins has proved his excellence on the track time after time, and although his current focus is on road racing, he will be looking to add to his track medal haul when the Olympics reach his hometown of London in 2012.

He was born in Belgium, the son of cyclist Gary Wiggins, but grew up in London. It was in the south of the capital, in Herne Hill, that he first experienced the excitement of a velodrome at the age of 12. By the time he was 18, in 1998, he was winning a silver medal in the team pursuit at the Commonwealth Games in Kuala Lumpur and looking good for Olympic success two years later.

**ABOVE** Bradley Wiggins taking part in a road race

Success duly arrived in Sydney. Riding with Paul Manning, Chris Newton and Bryan Steel in the men's team pursuit, Wiggins secured a bronze medal when the team overcame the French quartet in the medal round.

Bronze was not good enough, however, and Wiggins' ascent to world stardom continued with European and World Championship gold

medals. When the Olympics moved to Athens in 2004 he was at the top of his game, and he became the first Briton since Mary Rand in 1964 to win three medals at one Games.

Gold came in the individual pursuit, in which Wiggins accompanied teammate Rob Hayles into the medal round beat the Australian Brad McGee down into the silver position. Wiggins again found himself up against McGee in the gold medal match of the team pursuit event, but this time he had to be content with silver as the Aussies overcame the British foursome of Wiggins, Hayles, Manning and Steve Cummings. Australia was victorious again in the men's Madison, and the British duo of Wiggins and Hayles picked up bronze medals behind Switzerland.

Never mind. Athens had been a happy hunting ground for British cyclists and Wiggins had taken three of the nation's four medals. He was rewarded with an OBE on his return.

On to Beijing in 2008, where he successfully defended his title in the individual pursuit, setting a new Olympic record in the preliminary round as he did so. In the team pursuit, with Manning, Ed Clancy and Geraint Thomas, he went one better than in Athens by winning gold – and breaking the world record – as the Brits defeated Denmark.

If Athens had been good for British cycling, Beijing was fantastic: Britain topped the medals table with 14, eight of those being of the gold variety. All looks set for London 2012, for Wiggins and Britain.

# XXX Olympiad

When the opening ceremony to kick off the XXX Olympiad gets under way on 27 June 2012, London will have sealed its place as the first city to play host to the modern Olympic Games three times. The Games have taken their time to return to the UK capital, however: they were previously held in London in 1908 and 1948.

Long and loud were the celebrations in Singapore on 6 July 2005, when London got the nod from the International Olympic Committee, ahead of France, the bookies' favourite to win the Games. Headed by famed Olympian Sebastian Coe, London's bid team had convinced enough IOC members that they had the better prospects, but perhaps French president Jacques Chirac's ill-judged pronouncement on the British bid – "We can't trust people who have such bad food" – didn't help the French cause.

Coe – or Lord Coe, as he is officially known – immediately set about kick-starting the preparations for 2012 with the London Organising Committee for the Olympic Games (LOCOG). What the team have created for the Games and the Paralympics has transformed a vast swathe of London and promises to play host to an unforgettable 17 days of celebrations.

Some events will take place in existing and well-known London venues – such as Horse

**RIGHT** A general view of the scoreboard, showing that Lords will host the Archery during the 2012 London Olympics

Guards Parade (beach volleyball), Hyde Park (marathon swimming and triathlon), Wembley Stadium (football final), Wimbledon (tennis) and the Lord's cricket ground (archery) – but others will unfold in the brand new surroundings of the Olympic Park.

An area of more than two square kilometres, formerly contaminated industrial land in the east of London, has been transformed into a green space that will, after the Games have finished, provide a new, green quarter for people and wildlife. This zone is also where the Olympic Stadium and other facilities are to be found.

The spectacular, 80,000-capacity Olympic Stadium is, the organisers say, the most sustainable such facility ever built. It uses low-carbon concrete and 75 per cent less steel than comparable stadiums, and recycled gas pipes have even been used in the arena's top ring. The stadium, which will showcase the athletics element of the Games as well as the opening and closing ceremonies, is situated on an island site in the south of the Olympic Park, so spectators will arrive via one of five bridges. After the Olympic circus moves on, the capacity will be reduced and West Ham United Football Club will take up residency.

The Aquatics Centre, which forms the gateway to the Park, is another permanent facility, although it too will take on a different form after the Olympics. Most spectators will be seated in temporary wings of the structure, which will be removed afterwards with the spectator capacity being reduced from 17,500 to 2,500.

The Centre features a 50-metre competition pool, a 25-metre diving pool, a 50-metre warm-up pool and a 'dry' warm-up area for divers. Water polo will take place in a temporary structure next

door. The whole venue features a wave-like roof that is 160 metres long and 80 metres wide – a longer single span than that of Heathrow Airport's Terminal 5 building.

The track cycling at London 2012 will take place in the Velodrome which is, say the organisers, the most sustainable venue in the Olympic Park. The venue is entirely naturally ventilated and makes the best possible use of natural light, and the vast amount of timber used in construction was certified by the Forest Stewardship Council. Between the two tiers of seating – housing a total of 7,000 spectators – is a glass wall that gives people

inside a 360-degree view of the Olympic Park, and allows those outside to watch the sporting action taking place within.

The Velodrome's 'back of house' area is to be shared with the venues for basketball and BMX. The Basketball Arena will welcome up to 12,000 spectators during the Games, and will also host the final stages of the handball competition. One of the largest temporary venues erected for any Games, it will be taken down after 2012.

The 400-metre BMX Track, however, will serve as a community facility after the Games, albeit in a different form. During the Olympics, it will seat 6,000 BMX fans while afterwards it will form part of a Velo Park run by Lee Valley Regional Park Authority.

London's Hockey Centre will be a temporary structure with two pitches. Hockey's popularity in the Olympic schedule means the 16,000 seats will be fully occupied, but after the Games the Hockey Centre will move to the north of the Olympic Park, where it will join the group of facilities known as Eton Manor.

This is where, once the Olympics have

finished, a range of sporting facilities, for local and regional communities, will be located. They will include the Hockey Centre and a tennis centre with four indoor and six outdoor courts. During the Games, however, the Eton Manor site will offer training facilities for competitors in aquatics events: three 50-metre pools for swimmers and smaller pools for synchronised swimmers and water polo players.

The fencing element of the modern pentathlon and most of the handball events will take place in the Handball Arena, a 7,000-capacity facility that features more than 3,000 square metres of external copper cladding – most of it recycled. After the Games, it will be adapted to form a multi-sports venue for community use, athlete training and a variety of events.

The last of the new venues in the Olympic Park is the Water Polo area, which will be dismantled afterwards to be used in other UK locations.

But a host of other sites, inside and outside London, will also see Olympic action. In London, they will include the ExCeL (combat sports, table tennis, weightlifting) and Earls Court (volleyball) exhibition venues, Greenwich Park (equestrian events), Hampton Court palace

**FAR LEFT** An aerial view of the construction work for the London 2012 Olympic Games

**LEFT** Construction work in Stratford, the site of the Olympic Park for the 2012 Olympics

(road cycling), North Greenwich Arena (artistic gymnastics, trampoline, basketball), The Mall (marathons, race walking and road cycling), the Royal Artillery Barracks (shooting) and Wembley Arena (badminton and rhythmic gymnastics).

The rest of the UK will get a piece of the Olympic action, too. Football matches will take place in the City of Coventry Stadium, Cardiff's Millennium Stadium, Old Trafford in Manchester, Glasgow's Hampden Park and St James' Park in Newcastle upon Tyne, for example. The 2.2 kilometre Eton Dorney Centre, near Windsor in Berkshire, will host the rowing events, while the challenging paths, climbs and descents of Hadleigh Farm in Essex will face the mountain bikers.

Not too far away, in the Lee Valley White Water Centre, competitors in the canoe slalom will be put through their paces, while waters of a rather smoother nature at Weymouth and

Portland, in Dorset, will test the Olympic sailors.

We have not yet touched on two sites of major importance to any Olympic Games: the athletes' village and the media centre. The village, situated in the Olympic Park, will consist of apartments for approximately 17,000 athletes, together with shops, restaurants, medical, media and leisure facilities and plenty of open spaces. After the Games have moved on, the site will be transformed into 2,800 new homes. The International Broadcast Centre and Main Press Centre, in the north-west corner of the Park, feature 29,000 square metres of 'green' office space and will be used as business space after the Games. There will also be a 12,000 square metre catering village that is expected to serve 50,000 meals every day during the Olympics.

Let us not forget that the 2012 London Olympics will be accompanied by the city's Cultural Olympiad – more than 500 events spread over four years – and the Summer Paralympic Games, which will have 20 sports on view.

It all adds up to a spectacle the like of which the UK has never seen before – and one that promises to leave a rich legacy.

**LEFT** Mirtus Yifter brushes shoulders with a competitor before passing him and claiming victory in the men's 5,000m at the 1980 Olympic Games in Moscow

at,
a
the
ing

nich
n the
én of

of his
etres.
came
rising
pia, he
team

ycott
te in
cow

Games of 1980. The final of the 10,000 metres was dominated by the Ethiopian runners, with only Virén and his Finnish team mate Maaninka staying in contention. With 300 metres remaining, Yifter sprinted clear to take his first Olympic gold.

After his 1972 debacle he easily qualified for the 5,000 metres final. At 4,000 metres all 12 finalists were still together, Yifter apparently caught in the middle with countryman Mohammed Kadir in front of him.

With only 300 metres to the finish, Kadir looked round and with the wave of a hand stepped aside, allowing Yifter to unleash the sprint that had earned him the nickname Yifter the Shifter. Powering away, he crossed the line first to take the gold medal that had eluded him eight years before.

# Zátopek

Zátopek

**MIDDLE** Emil Zátopek leads in front of French Alain Mimoun and Herbert Schade during the Olympic 5000m in Helsinki

A carpenter's son, Emil Zátopek was born in Koprivince, Czechoslovakia in 1922. His athletic prowess was noted and encouraged when he joined the army in 1944, and the young lieutenant Zátopek was sent to the 1948 London Olympics.

Viljo Heino was expected to take victory in the 10,000 metres, but a ferocious pace set by Zátopek forced the Finn to drop out from exhaustion. Zátopek lapped all but two runners to take the gold medal. Three days later, he competed in the 5,000 metres final, securing a silver medal.

Zátopek's greatest achievements occurred at the 1952 Helsinki Olympics. Psychologically, he had won the 10,000 metres before it started, the other competitors standing back to allow him to choose his place on the line. Zátopek set the pace, forcing his opponents into s gold r

F 10,00( betwe Attac to t: On

# Yifter

Ethiopian Miruts Yifter was born in Adigr
Tigray Province. Having spent time as
carriage driver, it was not until he joined
Ethiopian Air Force that his talent for runr
was discovered.

Yifter made his Olympic debut at the Mu
Games of 1972, winning a bronze medal i
10,000 metres behind the great Lasse Vir
Finland.

However, arriving too late for the start
heat, he was eliminated from the 5,000 n
It has since been suggested that as Yifte
from Tigray, a region involved in an u
against the ruling dictatorship of Ethio
had been intentionally misinformed by
officials, preventing him from competing

Restricted by the pan-African be
of 1976, Yifter was unable to participa
Olympic competition again until the Mos

submission until he was on his own, a
medal already won.

...ur days later, in the closing laps of the
...0 metres final, a fierce battle ensued
...een Zátopek and three other athletes.
...king on the final bend, he powered away
...ake his second gold medal of the Games.
...that same day his wife, Dana, won a gold

ABOVE Emil Zátopek
after receiving a silver
medal in the 5000m

medal in the javelin.

Never having run the distance, Zátopek then announced he would enter the marathon. Unsure about pace, he decided to run alongside record-holding Briton Jim Peters.

Fifteen kilometres into the race Peters, Zátopek and Swede Gustav Jansson held a formidable lead. Looking across at Peters, Zátopek asked if the pace was good enough. An exhausted Peters, trying to save face, replied "too slow".

A few yards further on, Zátopek accelerated, leaving Peters for dead. Jansson faded after 20 miles but Zátopek pressed on alone to finish two-and-a-half minutes clear of the field. He had achieved an amazing Olympic treble.

# Also available:

Our best-selling *Focus On* range.

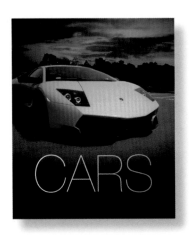

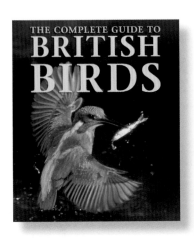

Our fact-packed *Picture This* range.

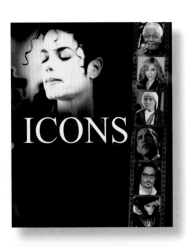
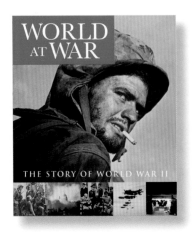
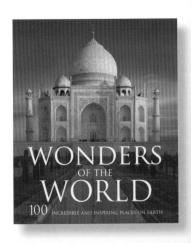